THE NICE & EASY COOKBOOK

FAVORITE RECIPES® PRESS

CREDITS

Great American Opportunities, Inc./Favorite Recipes® Press

President: Thomas F. McDow III

Editorial Manager: Mary Jane Blount
Editors: Georgia Brazil, Mary Cummings, Jane Hinshaw, Linda Jones,
Marian Sherman, Mary Wilson
Typography: Pam Newsome, Sara Anglin
Photography: Cover by National Pork Producers Council;
Hershey Foods Corporation; "M&M's" Chocolate Candies;
California Raisin Advisory Board; Oregon-Washington-California Pear Bureau

Published by: Favorite Recipes® Press, a division of
Great American Opportunities, Inc.
P. O. Box 305142
Nashville, TN 37230

Manufactured in the United States of America
First Printing: 1990, 34,000 copies
Second Printing: 1991, 27,000 copies

IT'S HAPPENING IN HOME ECONOMICS!!

Thomas F. McDow III
President

The traditional skills we associate with home economics education have been updated to serve American life today. For instance, "cooking" today includes quick, quality menu selection and easy meal preparation, time-saving recipes, cooking with convenience foods, adapting good nutrition to changing lifes-tyles, and involving other family members in food planning, selection and preparation.

And, in addition, home economics is addressing some of the most significant challenges facing America today—extended and single-parent families, home and family management, resource management and conservation, alcohol and drug abuse, consumer education, nutrition and health, teen pregnancy, AIDS and other sexually transmitted diseases.

We at Favorite Recipes® Press are proud to have worked hand-in-hand with home economics teachers publishing Home Economics Teachers Cookbooks for over 25 years. The sale of these books in community service projects has raised more than $50,000,000 in profits for home economics departments all across America.

We hope you continue to enjoy Home Economics Teachers Cookbooks, both the time-tested cookbooks on your shelf, and the new books in the series. The new cookbooks contain nutritional analysis, quick, easy and healthy dishes, many recipes that use basic ingredients already on hand, balanced meals and menus that are fun and easy to prepare by any member of the household, and many more features to fit modern American life-styles.

We hope, too, that you continue to support your local home economics teachers and students in their programs and activities. It is, indeed, happening in today's home economics!

Thomas F. McDow III
President

INTRODUCTION

In the past 20 years, Americans have launched a revolution in their approach to food that shows no signs of slowing down as we enter the last decade of the century. As a nation we're on the go, whether at work or during our leisure time, and even pre-schoolers seem to have schedules that a jet-setter would envy. The sheer amount of time we spend at the office, in the car, on the jogging track, in the classroom or running for a plane has changed the way we think about shopping for, preparing and eating meals.

Those days when Mom cooked all afternoon in preparation for a family dinner are over. Some of us are grateful for this change, some are not, but with more and more mothers working outside the home, and homemakers busy with dozens of extra activities, it's rare that we can spend as much time cooking as our mothers did.

If we've got less time to spend in the kitchen these days, though, our wish to serve appealing, nutritious food to our families has grown. More than ever we're all conscious of our diets, and more insistent than ever that the food we eat, if not necessarily slimming, be at least nutritionally valuable.

We want to give our families "real" meals—after all, how often can you order pizza without guilt? And we don't want to give up preparing all those treats we loved as kids: home baked bread, luscious desserts and great soups.

In The Nice & Easy Cookbook we've tried to cater to the needs of today's busy cook, who too often finds herself just home from work or errands with a hungry family on tap and half an hour to get dinner on the table. Or who needs to bake three dozen cookies for the Cub Scouts while simultaneously whipping up a Halloween costume. Or who finds out the office newcomer is coming home with Dad for dinner—an hour before they arrive. Sound familiar? We've all been there.

What you'll find in *The Nice & Easy Cookbook* are recipes that require an absolute minimum of hands-on preparation time, leaving you free to take care of the other 250 demands on your energy. These recipes also contain a limited number of ingredients, generally about half a dozen, to cut down on shopping and preparation time. These are usually ingredients you probably already have on your pantry shelves, or items you can keep on hand just for busier-than-usual times.

The techniques for preparing the recipes in *The Nice & Easy Cookbook* are just that: basic, simple preparation methods any cook can use, no matter how rushed she (or he) may be. You'll find no complicated instructions here, and only the most basic kitchen equipment, so there's no need to scour the darkest corners of the utensil drawers for that special cardamom grater or lemon zester.

In preparing these recipes you may well find ways to make them even quicker or easier, and come up with your own variations on our ideas. Go ahead! The key to great cooking for today's busy chef is flexibility—another ingredient in keeping things *Nice & Easy*.

TABLE OF CONTENTS

NUTRITIONAL ANALYSIS GUIDELINES

The editors have attempted to present these family recipes in a form that allows approximate nutritional values to be computed. Persons with dietary or health problems or whose diets require close monitoring should not rely solely on the nutritional information provided. They should consult their physician or a registered dietitian for specific information.

Abbreviations for Nutritional Analysis

Cal — Calories	T Fat — Total Fat	Sod — Sodium
Prot — Protein	Chol — Cholesterol	gr — gram
Carbo — Carbohydrates	Potas — Potassium	mg — milligram

Nutritional information for recipes is computed from values furnished by the United States Department of Agriculture Handbook. Many specialty items and new products now available on the market are not included in this handbook. However, producers of new products frequently publish nutritional information on each product's packaging and that information may be added, as applicable, for a more complete analysis. If the nutritional analysis notes the exclusion of a particular ingredient, check the package information.

Unless otherwise specified, the nutritional analysis of these recipes is based on all measurements being level.

- Artificial sweeteners vary in use and strength so should be used "to taste," using the recipe ingredients as a guideline.
- Artificial sweeteners using aspertame (NutraSweet and Equal) should not be used as a sweetener in recipes involving prolonged heating which reduces the sweet taste. For further information on the use of these sweeteners, refer to package information.
- Alcoholic ingredients have been analyzed for the basic ingredients, although cooking causes the evaporation of alcohol thus decreasing caloric content.
- Buttermilk, sour cream, and yogurt are commercial types.
- Cake mixes prepared using package directions include 3 eggs and $1/2$ cup oil.
- Chicken, cooked for boning and chopping, has been roasted; this method yields the lowest caloric values.
- Cottage cheese is cream-style with 4.2% creaming mixture. Dry-curd cottage cheese has no creaming mixture.
- Eggs are all large.
- Flour is unsifted all-purpose flour.
- Garnishes, serving suggestions and other optional additions and variations are not included in the analysis.
- Margarine and butter are regular, not whipped or presoftened.
- Milk is whole milk, 3.5% butterfat. Lowfat milk is 1% butterfat. Evaporated milk is whole milk with 60% of the water removed.
- Oil is any type of vegetable cooking oil. Shortening is hydrogenated vegetable shortening.
- Salt and other ingredients to taste as noted in the method have not been included in the nutritional analysis.
- If a choice of ingredients has been given, the nutritional analysis reflects the first option.

MICROWAVE BACON POLES

10 slices bacon
20 long thin breadsticks

Cut bacon into halves lengthwise. Wrap barber-pole fashion around breadsticks. Arrange on double thickness of paper towel in bottom of 9x13-inch baking dish. Cover with paper towel. Microwave on High for 10 to 13 minutes or until bacon is crisp, turning dish once. Yield: 20 servings.

Approx Per Serving:
Cal 124; Prot 4 g; Carbo 20 g; T Fat 3 g; Chol 3 mg; Potas 48 mg; Sod 598 mg.

Sandi Davison, Missouri

BEEFY CHEESE BALL

8 ounces cream cheese, softened
1 teaspoon prepared horseradish
1 teaspoon Worcestershire sauce
1 tablespoon lemon juice
1 tablespoon dry onion soup mix
1   4-ounce package dried beef, chopped

Combine first 5 ingredients in bowl; mix well. Fold in dried beef. Shape into ball. Chill until firm. Serve with crackers. Yield: 12 servings.

Approx Per Serving:
Cal 83; Prot 4 g; Carbo 1 g; T Fat 7 g; Chol 36 mg; Potas 72 mg; Sod 405 mg.

Tina Scott, Florida

DEVILED CHEESE BITES

8 ounces cream cheese, softened
1   2¼-ounce can deviled ham
1   12-ounce can pineapple tidbits, drained
¼ cup chopped chives

Blend cream cheese and ham in bowl. Drain pineapple on paper towels. Cut each tidbit into halves crosswise. Shape cream cheese mixture into balls around pineapple bits. Coat with chives. Chill until serving time. Yield: 30 servings.

Approx Per Serving:
Cal 37; Prot 1 g; Carbo 2 g; T Fat 3 g; Chol 9 mg; Potas 25 mg; Sod 42 mg.

Judy Stapleton, Illinois

HAM AND CHEESE BALL

1   4½-ounce can deviled ham

8 ounces cream cheese, softened

8 ounces Cheddar cheese, shredded

Shape deviled ham into ball. Mold cream cheese around ham ball. Roll in Cheddar cheese. Chill, wrapped in plastic wrap, until serving time. Serve with assorted crackers. Yield: 10 servings.

Approx Per Serving:
Cal 220; Prot 9 g; Carbo 1 g; T Fat 20 g;
Chol 56 mg; Potas 64 mg; Sod 373 mg.

Norma Carroll, Maryland

CRAB NIBBLES

1½ teaspoons mayonnaise

½ cup melted margarine

1   4-ounce jar Old English Cheddar cheese spread, softened

1   6-ounce can crab meat, well drained

½ teaspoon garlic salt

½ teaspoon seasoned salt

6 English muffins, split

Combine first 6 ingredients in bowl; mix well. Spread on muffin halves. Cut each half into 8 wedges. Place on baking sheet. Broil for 5 minutes or until bubbly. Yield: 72 servings.

Approx Per Serving:
Cal 31; Prot 1 g; Carbo 2 g; T Fat 2 g;
Chol 3 mg; Potas 41 mg; Sod 106 mg.

Peg Henderson, New York

ALOHA SPREAD

8 ounces cream cheese, softened

1 cup crushed pineapple

1 cup flaked coconut

1½ teaspoons ginger

2 teaspoons lemon juice

½ cup chopped pecans

Beat cream cheese in mixer bowl until light and fluffy. Add pineapple, coconut, ginger and lemon juice; mix well. Stir in pecans. Chill until serving time. Serve with assorted crackers or bite-sized fresh fruit. Yield: 24 servings.

Approx Per Serving:
Cal 75; Prot 1 g; Carbo 4 g; T Fat 6 g;
Chol 10 mg; Potas 44 mg; Sod 31 mg.

Myrtle Monroe, California

AMBROSIA FRUIT DIP

1 cup fruit-flavored yogurt

1/2 cup cream of coconut

1/4 cup chopped toasted pecans

Combine yogurt and cream of coconut in bowl; mix well. Stir in pecans. Chill in refrigerator. Serve with fresh fruit. Yield: 32 servings.

Approx Per Serving:
Cal 13; Prot 0 g; Carbo 2 g; T Fat 1 g; Chol 0 mg; Potas 18 mg; Sod 4 mg. Nutritional information does not include cream of coconut.

Cheryl Nelson, Ohio

ORANGE FRUIT DIP

1 6-ounce can frozen orange juice concentrate, thawed

1/4 cup milk

1 3-ounce package vanilla instant pudding mix

1/2 cup sour cream

Combine first 3 ingredients in mixer bowl. Beat for 2 minutes. Stir in sour cream. Chill for 2 hours. Serve with fruit. Yield: 32 servings.

Approx Per Serving:
Cal 27; Prot 0 g; Carbo 5 g; T Fat 1 g; Chol 2 mg; Potas 44 mg; Sod 21 mg.

Laurene Peterson, Indiana

DELICIOUS ARTICHOKE DIP

1 16-ounce can artichoke hearts, chopped

1 cup mayonnaise

1 cup Parmesan cheese

1/8 teaspoon garlic salt

Combine all ingredients in small casserole; mix well. Bake at 350 degrees for 15 minutes. Serve with taco chips. Yield: 48 servings.

Approx Per Serving:
Cal 50; Prot 1 g; Carbo 1 g; T Fat 5 g; Chol 4 mg; Potas 28 mg; Sod 113 mg.

Ho Johnson, Georgia

MINCED CLAM DIP

1 package dry vegetable soup mix

2 cups sour cream

1 7-ounce can minced clams, drained

Combine all ingredients in bowl; mix well. Chill until serving time. Yield: 48 servings.

Approx Per Serving:
Cal 28; Prot 1 g; Carbo 2 g; T Fat 2 g; Chol 7 mg; Potas 30 mg; Sod 126 mg.

Elsie Kennedy, Texas

Ginger Dip

12 ounces cream cheese, softened	Combine all ingredients in bowl; mix well. Chill until serving time. Yield: 48 servings.
1 cup drained crushed pineapple	*Approx Per Serving:*
2 tablespoons lemon juice	Cal 48; Prot 1 g; Carbo 2 g; T Fat 4 g;
1 teaspoon ground ginger	Chol 8 mg; Potas 28 mg; Sod 21 mg.
1 3-ounce can flaked coconut	*Jane Skaryd, Ohio*
3/4 cup chopped pecans	

Guacamole

3 large avocados, mashed	Combine first 5 ingredients in bowl; mix well. Chill for 1 hour. Serve on lettuce-lined serving plate; top with olives. Yield: 64 servings.
1 tablespoon minced onion	
1 teaspoon celery salt	*Approx Per Serving:*
1 teaspoon garlic powder	Cal 16; Prot 0 g; Carbo 1 g; T Fat 2 g;
3 tablespoons picante sauce	Chol 0 mg; Potas 53 mg; Sod 45 mg.
1/4 cup chopped black olives	*Lydia Bowers, Arizona*

Microwave Mexican Party Dip

1 16-ounce can tamales	Mash tamales with fork in 1 1/2-quart glass baking dish. Add soup and chili; mix well. Microwave on High until heated through. Serve with tortilla chips. Yield: 8 servings.
1 10-ounce can cheese soup	
1 16-ounce can chili with beans	Nutritional information for this recipe is not available.
	Christy Jones, Michigan

Piña Colada Fruit Dip

1 3-ounce package coconut instant pudding mix	Combine all ingredients in blender container. Process for 30 seconds. Chill for several hours. Serve with fresh fruit. Yield: 40 servings.
3/4 cup milk	
1 8-ounce can crushed pineapple, drained	*Approx Per Serving:*
1/2 cup vanilla yogurt	Cal 16; Prot 0 g; Carbo 3 g; T Fat 0 g; Chol 1 mg; Potas 18 mg; Sod 18 mg.
	Phyllis Jackson, Maine

CREAMY SHRIMP DIP

½ cup chili sauce

8 ounces cream cheese, softened

½ cup mayonnaise

¼ cup chopped onion

2 teaspoons prepared horseradish

1 6-ounce can shrimp, rinsed, drained

Blend chili sauce and cream cheese in bowl. Add remaining ingredients; mix well. Chill, covered, for 1 hour. Serve with chips. Yield: 40 servings.

Approx Per Serving:
Cal 49; Prot 2 g; Carbo 1 g; T Fat 4 g; Chol 15 mg; Potas 32 mg; Sod 86 mg.

Gina Tipton, Minnesota

DEVILED ROLLS

1 8-count can refrigerator crescent rolls

½ cup butter, softened

2 4-ounce cans deviled ham

Unroll crescent roll dough. Spread with butter and deviled ham. Cut into 16 triangles. Roll up starting from wide end. Shape into crescents on baking sheet. Bake at 350 degrees for 15 minutes or until brown. Yield: 16 servings.

Approx Per Serving:
Cal 131; Prot 2 g; Carbo 7 g; T Fat 11 g; Chol 21 mg; Potas 54 mg; Sod 293 mg.

Mattie Roberts, Michigan

FROSTED GRAPES

1 pound grapes

1 egg white, slightly beaten

½ cup sugar

Brush clusters of grapes with egg white. Place sugar and grapes in bag; shake to coat. Place on wire rack. Let stand until dry. Arrange on serving platter. Yield: 10 servings.

Nutritional information for this recipe is not available.

Ellen Long, Ohio

HAM PINWHEELS

4 ounces bleu cheese, softened

4 ounces cream cheese, softened

1/4 cup butter, softened

4   1-ounce slices boiled ham

Combine cheeses and butter in bowl; mix well. Spread on ham slices. Roll each slice as for jelly roll. Chill in refrigerator. Cut into thin slices. Serve on crackers. Yield: 24 servings.

Approx Per Serving:
Cal 57; Prot 2 g; Carbo 0 g; T Fat 5 g;
Chol 16 mg; Potas 34 mg; Sod 156 mg.

Etta Strand, Wisconsin

HAWAIIAN DELIGHT

1 cup whipping cream

1 cup sour cream

2 tablespoons confectioners' sugar

6 firm bananas

1   8-ounce can flaked coconut

Whip cream in bowl until soft peaks form. Fold in sour cream and confectioners' sugar. Cut bananas into 2-inch slices. Dip in cream mixture. Coat with coconut. Place on serving plate. Chill until serving time. Yield: 18 servings.

Approx Per Serving:
Cal 166; Prot 1 g; Carbo 15 g; T Fat 12 g;
Chol 24 mg; Potas 219 mg; Sod 15 mg.

Dorothy Wuertz, California

GOURMET MUSHROOMS

36 medium mushrooms

8 ounces Neufchâtel cheese, softened

1   7-ounce can crab meat, drained

Garlic powder to taste

1/2 teaspoon lemon juice

3/4 cup shredded Cheddar cheese

Wash mushrooms; discard stems. Place caps on baking sheet. Combine Neufchâtel cheese, crab meat and seasonings in bowl; mix well. Fold in Cheddar cheese. Spoon into mushroom caps. Bake at 350 degrees until light brown. Serve immediately. Yield: 36 servings.

Approx Per Serving:
Cal 32; Prot 2 g; Carbo 0 g; T Fat 2 g;
Chol 12 mg; Potas 45 mg; Sod 58 mg.

Dottie Morton, Kentucky

Parmesan Crisps

8 slices white bread, crusts trimmed

¾ cup Parmesan cheese

¾ teaspoon chili powder

¾ cup melted butter

Cut each bread slice into 6 sticks; place on baking sheet. Bake at 375 degrees for 3 minutes. Combine cheese and chili powder in shallow dish. Dip bread sticks in butter; coat with cheese mixture. Return to baking sheet. Bake for 3 minutes longer or until golden brown. Serve warm. Yield: 48 servings.

Approx Per Serving:
Cal 44; Prot 1 g; Carbo 2 g; T Fat 3 g;
Chol 9 mg; Potas 8 mg; Sod 72 mg.

Louise Moore, Texas

Sausage Balls

1 pound hot sausage

3 cups buttermilk baking mix

8 ounces sharp Cheddar cheese, shredded

Combine all ingredients in bowl; mix well. Shape into small balls. Place on baking sheet. Bake at 400 degrees for 15 minutes. Serve hot. May be frozen before baking. Yield: 36 servings.

Approx Per Serving:
Cal 123; Prot 4 g; Carbo 7 g; T Fat 9 g;
Chol 15 mg; Potas 47 mg; Sod 255 mg.

Anne Cameron, New Jersey

Glazed Sausage Bites

1 cup apple jelly

2 tablespoons mustard

2 tablespoons prepared horseradish

24 cocktail sausages

Combine apple jelly, mustard and horseradish in skillet; mix well. Bring to a boil. Add sausages. Simmer until sausages are heated through and glazed. Serve hot. Yield: 24 servings.

Approx Per Serving:
Cal 143; Prot 4 g; Carbo 9 g; T Fat 11 g;
Chol 20 mg; Potas 71 mg; Sod 249 mg.

Marsha Harmon, North Carolina

BAKED CRAB SPREAD

2 7-ounce cans crab meat, drained

8 ounces cream cheese, softened

1/4 cup slivered almonds

2 tablespoons milk

2 tablespoons minced onion

1 teaspoon prepared horseradish

Combine all ingredients in bowl; mix well. Spoon into 1-quart casserole. Bake at 375 degrees for 20 minutes. Serve hot with crackers. Yield: 48 servings.

Approx Per Serving:
Cal 29; Prot 2 g; Carbo 0 g; T Fat 2 g;
Chol 13 mg; Potas 44 mg; Sod 42 mg.

Mary Henderson, Mississippi

HAM SPREAD

8 ounces cream cheese, softened

1/4 cup mayonnaise

2 7-ounce cans chunky ham

1 tablespoon minced onion

1/4 teaspoon dry mustard

Combine all ingredients in bowl; mix well. Serve with crackers or vegetables. Yield: 32 servings.

Approx Per Serving:
Cal 55; Prot 3 g; Carbo 0 g; T Fat 5 g;
Chol 13 mg; Potas 51 mg; Sod 189 mg.

Lisa Edwardson, Kansas

JEZEBEL SPREAD

1 8-ounce jar pineapple preserves

1 8-ounce jar apple jelly

1 2-ounce jar horseradish

1/4 cup mustard

1/4 teaspoon pepper

16 ounces cream cheese

Combine first 5 ingredients in saucepan; mix well. Cook over medium heat for 5 minutes, stirring constantly. Cool. Chill in refrigerator. Serve over cream cheese with crackers. Yield: 32 servings.

Approx Per Serving:
Cal 90; Prot 1 g; Carbo 11 g; T Fat 5 g;
Chol 16 mg; Potas 37 mg; Sod 70 mg.

Joyce Nelson, Montana

SALMON SPREAD

1 7-ounce can pink salmon

8 ounces cream cheese, softened

Garlic powder and onion powder to taste

1/2 cup finely chopped celery

Combine salmon and cream cheese in bowl; mix well. Add remaining ingredients; mix well. Serve with crackers. Yield: 32 servings.

Approx Per Serving:
Cal 35; Prot 2 g; Carbo 0 g; T Fat 3 g;
Chol 10 mg; Potas 37 mg; Sod 56 mg.

Margaret Carrier, Illinois

STUFFED BABY TOMATOES

2 baskets cherry tomatoes
1 cup mayonnaise
1/4 cup Parmesan cheese
1 tablespoon horseradish
2 tablespoons minced onion
1/2 cup chopped fresh spinach, puréed

Cut tomatoes into halves; scoop out and discard pulp. Combine remaining ingredients in bowl; mix well. Spoon into tomato halves. Chill until serving time. Yield: 48 servings.

Approx Per Serving:
Cal 39; Prot 0 g; Carbo 1 g; T Fat 4 g;
Chol 3 mg; Potas 49 mg; Sod 36 mg.

Carla Franklin, Alabama

MICROWAVE CHEESY TORTILLA ROLL-UPS

1 1/2 cups shredded sharp Cheddar cheese
3 tablespoons dry onion soup mix
1/2 cup sour cream
1/4 cup Parmesan cheese
12 flour tortillas

Combine first 4 ingredients in bowl; mix well. Spread on tortillas; roll as for jelly roll. Cut each into 3 pieces; secure with toothpicks. Arrange on plate. Microwave on High for 1 minute or until heated through. Yield: 36 servings.

Approx Per Serving:
Cal 65; Prot 2 g; Carbo 7 g; T Fat 3 g;
Chol 7 mg; Potas 25 mg; Sod 138 mg.

Bonnie Ellis, Tennessee

MAPLENUTS

1 pound raw peanuts
1 cup sugar
1/2 cup water
1 tablespoon maple flavoring

Combine all ingredients in heavy skillet. Cook over high heat until water evaporates, stirring constantly. Spread on baking sheet. Bake at 300 degrees for 30 minutes. Yield: 16 servings.

Approx Per Serving:
Cal 208; Prot 7 g; Carbo 18 g; T Fat 14 g;
Chol 0 mg; Potas 197 mg; Sod 3 mg.

Holly Shilling, New York

Recipe for this photograph is on page 145.

EASY AND FUN PARTIES

Make it nibbles and punch or a full meal.

Microwave Bacon Poles, 8

Crab Nibbles, 9

Ambrosia Fruit Dip, 10

Fresh Fruit

Snack Crackers, 19

Guacamole, 11

Tortilla Chips

Fiesta Tossed Salad, 40

Crock•Pot Chili, 53

Hot Buttered Flour Tortillas

Microwave Apple Topping on Ice Cream, 113

Assorted Hot or Cold Beverages

People Puppy Chow

1/2 cup margarine

1 cup peanut butter

2 cups milk chocolate chips

1 12-ounce box Crispix cereal

4 cups confectioners' sugar

Melt first 3 ingredients in saucepan, stirring constantly. Pour over cereal in large bowl; mix gently. Pour half the confectioners' sugar in bag. Add coated cereal. Shake well. Add remaining confectioners' sugar. Shake to coat completely. Yield: 40 servings.

Approx Per Serving:
Cal 174; Prot 3 g; Carbo 23 g; T Fat 9 g;
Chol 0 mg; Potas 85 mg; Sod 125 mg.

Mary Weise, Idaho

Sweet Treats

3 cups dried banana chips

3 cups thin pretzel sticks

1 1/2 cups raisins

1 1/2 cups "M&M's" Peanut Chocolate Candies

Combine banana chips, pretzels, raisins and candies in bowl; mix well. Store in airtight container. May substitute sesame sticks for banana chips or use "M&M's" Plain Chocolate Candies if preferred. Yield: 8 cups.

Photograph for this recipe is on page 35.

Snack Crackers

1 cup corn oil

1 envelope dry ranch salad dressing mix

1/2 teaspoon garlic powder

1 teaspoon dillweed

2 12-ounce packages oyster crackers

Combine first 4 ingredients in bowl; mix well. Add crackers; mix well. Let stand for 1 hour or longer. Store in airtight container.
Yield: 24 servings.

Approx Per Serving:
Cal 200; Prot 3 g; Carbo 20 g; T Fat 12 g;
Chol 0 mg; Potas 34 mg; Sod 355 mg.
Nutritional information does not include salad dressing mix.

Harriet Malone, Maryland

Toasty Onion Snacks

3/4 cup chopped onion

1/2 cup mayonnaise

1/4 cup Parmesan cheese

24 crackers

Combine onion, mayonnaise and cheese in bowl; mix well. Spread on crackers. Place on baking sheet. Broil just until golden brown. Serve hot. Yield: 24 servings.

Approx Per Serving:
Cal 51; Prot 1 g; Carbo 3 g; T Fat 4 g;
Chol 4 mg; Potas 15 mg; Sod 81 mg.

Mary Jane Parkinson, California

Cheesy Rye Nibbles

6 ounces cream cheese, softened

1 envelope dry Italian salad dressing mix

5 slices rye bread

Combine cream cheese and salad dressing mix in bowl; mix well. Spread on bread slices. Cut each slice into quarters. Top with cucumber slices, olive slices or thinly sliced green onions, if desired. Yield: 20 servings.

Approx Per Serving:
Cal 53; Prot 1 g; Carbo 5 g; T Fat 3 g;
Chol 9 mg; Potas 34 mg; Sod 87 mg.
Nutritional information does not
include salad dressing mix.

Eleanor Thomas, Tennessee

Autumn Leaf Punch

3 cups apricot nectar

3 cups apple cider

3 tablespoons sugar

3 tablespoons lemon juice

8 whole cloves

Combine all ingredients in saucepan. Bring to a boil, stirring until sugar dissolves. Strain. Serve hot. May store in refrigerator and reheat if desired. Yield: 6 servings.

Approx Per Serving:
Cal 146; Prot 1 g; Carbo 37 g; T Fat 0 g;
Chol 0 mg; Potas 300 mg; Sod 8 mg.

Joyce Miller, Florida

BANANA SHAKE

1 cup cold milk
1 banana, chopped
2 teaspoons sugar
1 egg

Combine all ingredients in blender container. Process until frothy. Serve for breakfast with cinnamon toast. Yield: 1 serving.

Approx Per Serving:
Cal 366; Prot 15 g; Carbo 47 g; T Fat 14 g; Chol 307 mg; Potas 843 mg; Sod 172 mg.

Kathy McAllister, South Dakota

CHERRY FRAPPÉ

2 4-ounce jars red maraschino cherries
1 pint vanilla ice cream, softened
2 pints orange sherbet
Crushed ice

Combine cherries with juice, vanilla ice cream and half the sherbet in blender container. Process until smooth. Pour into glasses half-filled with ice. Top with scoops of remaining sherbet. Garnish with mint. Serve with straws. Yield: 6 servings.

Approx Per Serving:
Cal 314; Prot 3 g; Carbo 61 g; T Fat 7 g; Chol 29 mg; Potas 265 mg; Sod 98 mg.

Phyllis Lee, Washington

CREAMY PARTY PUNCH

1 quart vanilla ice cream
1 quart strawberry ice cream
1 46-ounce can Hawaiian punch
1 46-ounce can pineapple-orange juice
1 46-ounce can cranberry juice
2 quarts ginger ale, chilled

Place scoops of ice cream in punch bowl. Mix Hawaiian punch and juices in large container. Pour over ice cream. Add ginger ale just before serving; stir gently. Yield: 25 servings.

Approx Per Serving:
Cal 193; Prot 2 g; Carbo 37 g; T Fat 5 g; Chol 19 mg; Potas 130 mg; Sod 57 mg.

Linda Mercer, Alabama

GOLDEN PARTY PUNCH

1	12-ounce can frozen orange juice concentrate
1	12-ounce can frozen lemonade concentrate
1	12-ounce can apricot nectar
1	46-ounce can pineapple juice
	2 quarts orange sherbet, softened
	1 quart ginger ale, chilled

Reconstitute orange juice and lemonade concentrates, using package directions. Combine with apricot nectar and pineapple juice in large container. Add sherbet; mix well. Pour over ice in punch bowl. Add ginger ale just before serving. Yield: 40 servings.

Approx Per Serving:
Cal 125; Prot 1 g; Carbo 30 g; T Fat 1 g;
Chol 0 mg; Potas 161 mg; Sod 5 mg.

Edith Davis, New Hampshire

HULA MILK SHAKE

2 large ripe bananas
2/3 cup cold milk
2/3 cup cold pineapple juice
Juice of 1 lime
Crushed ice

Combine all ingredients in 1-quart shaker. Shake vigorously. Serve immediately. Yield: 2 servings.

Approx Per Serving:
Cal 207; Prot 4 g; Carbo 44 g; T Fat 3 g;
Chol 11 mg; Potas 695 mg; Sod 36 mg.

Candy Chandler, Iowa

LEMONADE REFRESHER

1	46-ounce can orange-pineapple drink
1	12-ounce can frozen lemonade concentrate
1	28-ounce bottle of ginger ale
	1 pint orange sherbet

Combine orange-pineapple drink, lemonade concentrate and 2 lemonade cans water in pitcher; mix well. Chill in refrigerator. Stir in ginger ale. Scoop orange sherbet into glasses; add ginger ale mixture. Yield: 10 servings.

Approx Per Serving:
Cal 208; Prot 2 g; Carbo 50 g; T Fat 1 g;
Chol 3 mg; Potas 124 mg; Sod 29 mg.

Alice Nelson, Utah

Orange Nog

1/3 cup frozen orange juice concentrate

1 pint vanilla ice cream

1 egg

2 cups milk

Nutmeg to taste

Combine orange juice concentrate, ice cream and egg in mixer bowl. Beat until blended. Add milk gradually, beating constantly. Serve in chilled mugs. Sprinkle with nutmeg.
Yield: 4 servings.

Approx Per Serving:
Cal 267; Prot 8 g; Carbo 31 g; T Fat 13 g;
Chol 114 mg; Potas 466 mg; Sod 127 mg.

Martha Welch, Mississippi

Triple Citrus Punch

2 quarts cranberry juice, chilled

1   12-ounce can frozen orange juice concentrate

1   6-ounce can frozen lemonade concentrate

1   6-ounce can frozen limeade concentrate

1 quart ginger ale, chilled

Combine all ingredients in large punch bowl. Serve over ice. Yield: 25 serving.

Approx Per Serving:
Cal 128; Prot 1 g; Carbo 32 g; T Fat 0 g;
Chol 0 mg; Potas 140 mg; Sod 2 mg.

Marlene Swanson, Vermont

Hot Mulled Cider

1/2 cup packed brown sugar

2 quarts apple cider

1 teaspoon whole allspice

1 teaspoon whole cloves

1 stick cinnamon

Pinch of nutmeg

Combine brown sugar and cider in saucepan. Tie spices in cheesecloth. Add to cider. Simmer, covered, for 20 minutes. Remove spices. Pour into mugs. Garnish with orange slices.
Yield: 8 servings.

Approx Per Serving:
Cal 109; Prot 0 g; Carbo 28 g; T Fat 0 g;
Chol 0 mg; Potas 195 mg; Sod 10 mg.

Ruth Roman, Iowa

Hot Spiced Cranberry Glog

2 quarts cranapple juice

1 quart water

1 cup packed brown sugar

3 sticks cinnamon

1 teaspoon allspice

1 teaspoon whole cloves

Combine all ingredients in saucepan. Bring to a boil. Strain into mugs. Yield: 16 servings.

Approx Per Serving:
Cal 136; Prot 0 g; Carbo 35 g; T Fat 0 g;
Chol 0 mg; Potas 81 mg; Sod 9 mg.

Wanda Wheeler, Montana

Italian Coffee

1/2 cup evaporated milk

2 tablespoons confectioners' sugar

1/4 teaspoon vanilla extract

1/4 teaspoon cinnamon

6 cups hot strong coffee

Chill evaporated milk in mixer bowl in freezer until partially frozen. Add confectioners' sugar, vanilla and cinnamon. Beat until thick and fluffy. Fill cups 1/3 full. Add hot coffee. Garnish with grated chocolate. Yield: 6 servings.

Approx Per Serving:
Cal 38; Prot 2 g; Carbo 5 g; T Fat 2 g;
Chol 6 mg; Potas 194 mg; Sod 28 mg.

Terri Donovan, Virginia

Gold Coast Coffee

1 cup instant cocoa drink mix

1/3 cup instant coffee granules

4 cups boiling water

1 cup whipping cream, whipped

Nutmeg to taste

Combine cocoa mix, coffee granules and boiling water in coffee pot; mix well. Pour into cups. Top with whipped cream and nutmeg. Yield: 6 servings.

Approx Per Serving:
Cal 273; Prot 6 g; Carbo 33 g; T Fat 16 g;
Chol 56 mg; Potas 439 mg; Sod 202 mg.

Georgia Case, Virginia

Speedy
Soups, Salads
& Sandwiches

BEEF AND BROCCOLI CHOWDER

1 pound ground beef

1 medium onion, chopped

1 package Hamburger Helper
potatoes au gratin

2 medium carrots, chopped

¹⁄₄ teaspoon dry mustard

Salt and pepper to taste

6 cups water

1   10-ounce package frozen
chopped broccoli, thawed

Brown ground beef with onion in skillet, stirring frequently; drain. Add potatoes, carrots, seasonings and water. Simmer, covered, for 15 minutes, stirring occasionally. Add broccoli. Cook, covered, for 10 minutes longer.
Yield: 8 servings.

Approx Per Serving:
Cal 139; Prot 12 g; Carbo 5 g; T Fat 8 g;
Chol 37 mg; Potas 281 mg; Sod 48 mg.
Nutritional information does not include
potatoes au gratin.

Martha Cox, Georgia

BROCCOLI AND CHEDDAR SOUP

5¹⁄₂ cups milk

1¹⁄₂ cups chopped broccoli

3 tablespoons chopped onion

2 tablespoons butter, softened

1 tablespoon flour

2 cups shredded Cheddar
cheese

Salt and pepper to taste

Bring milk just to the simmering point in saucepan. Add broccoli and onion. Cook for 10 minutes or until vegetables are tender. Stir in mixture of butter and flour. Cook until thickened, stirring constantly. Remove from heat. Stir in cheese and seasonings. Yield: 8 servings.

Approx Per Serving:
Cal 252; Prot 13 g; Carbo 10 g; T Fat 18 g;
Chol 60 mg; Potas 314 mg; Sod 274 mg.

Sarah Tomlin, Virginia

BEEFY VEGETABLE SOUP

1 pound ground beef

1 medium onion, chopped

1   28-ounce can vegetable
juice cocktail

3 cups frozen mixed vegetables

Pepper to taste

Brown ground beef with onion in skillet, stirring frequently; drain. Stir in remaining ingredients. Simmer for 15 minutes or until vegetables are tender. Yield: 4 servings.

Approx Per Serving:
Cal 362; Prot 27 g; Carbo 30 g; T Fat 17 g;
Chol 74 mg; Potas 932 mg; Sod 838 mg.

Georgia Jacobs, Illinois

Cheesy Cauliflower Soup

1   10-ounce package frozen cauliflower
2 cups milk
2 tablespoons butter
1 cup instant potato flakes
2 teaspoons instant onion flakes
1 can chicken broth
8 ounces Velveeta cheese

Cook cauliflower using package directions; do not drain. Purée cauliflower with liquid in blender container. Heat milk and butter in saucepan; do not boil. Stir in potato flakes and onion. Add to cauliflower. Process until smooth. Pour into saucepan. Add broth. Simmer for 10 minutes. Add cheese. Cook until cheese melts, stirring constantly. Serve with toasted croutons. Yield: 6 servings.

Approx Per Serving:
Cal 364; Prot 16 g; Carbo 34 g; T Fat 19 g;
Chol 58 mg; Potas 508 mg; Sod 823 mg.

Sarah Austin, Arkansas

Cheese Soup

1 cup chopped onion
1 cup chopped celery
4 chicken bouillon cubes
1½ quarts water
2½ cups frozen hashed brown potatoes
1   10-ounce package frozen mixed vegetables
2 cans cream of chicken soup
1½ pounds Velveeta cheese

Combine first 6 ingredients in Crock•Pot. Cook on Low for 8 hours. Add soup and cheese. Cook on High until cheese melts. Stir before serving. Yield: 12 servings.

Approx Per Serving:
Cal 369; Prot 17 g; Carbo 22 g; T Fat 25 g;
Chol 58 mg; Potas 404 mg; Sod 1618 mg.

Mary Christman, California

Crock•Pot Clam Chowder

4 cans cream of potato soup
2   12-ounce cans evaporated milk
2   6-ounce cans chopped clams
¾ cup chopped carrots
1 cup chopped onion
4 ounces bacon, chopped

Combine all ingredients in Crock•Pot. Cook on Low for 8 hours. Yield: 6 servings.

Approx Per Serving:
Cal 535; Prot 31 g; Carbo 36 g; T Fat 29 g;
Chol 135 mg; Potas 1099 mg; Sod 2171 mg.

Betsy Washington, New Jersey

CREAMY CORN CHOWDER

3 medium potatoes, peeled, chopped

1 small onion, chopped

1/4 cup margarine

1 cup water

1 16-ounce can corn, drained

4 cups milk

Salt and pepper to taste

Combine potatoes, onion, margarine and water in saucepan. Simmer for 15 minutes or until potatoes are tender. Add corn and milk. Simmer for 15 minutes. Add seasonings. Yield: 8 servings.

Approx Per Serving:
Cal 259; Prot 7 g; Carbo 37 g; T Fat 10 g; Chol 17 mg; Potas 593 mg; Sod 256 mg.

Lee Lawrence, Kentucky

CHUCK WAGON CHOWDER

2 pounds ground beef

1 small onion, chopped

1/2 green bell pepper, chopped

1 29-ounce can tomatoes

Chili powder and salt to taste

2 cups uncooked noodles

Brown ground beef with onion and green pepper in skillet, stirring frequently; drain. Add tomatoes and seasonings. Bring to a boil. Add noodles; reduce heat. Simmer, covered, for 30 minutes, stirring frequently. Yield: 6 servings.

Approx Per Serving:
Cal 428; Prot 33 g; Carbo 24 g; T Fat 23 g; Chol 99 mg; Potas 748 mg; Sod 314 mg.

Missy Finch, Ohio

EASY ITALIAN MEATBALL SOUP

8 ounces ground beef

1/2 cup chopped onion

1 clove of garlic, minced

Oregano to taste

1 can bean and bacon soup

1 can minestrone soup

1 soup can water

1 16-ounce can kidney beans, drained

2 cups coarsely chopped cabbage

Salt and pepper to taste

Shape ground beef into small balls. Brown on all sides in skillet. Remove meatballs. Add onion, garlic and oregano to pan drippings. Sauté until onion is tender. Combine meatballs, sautéed vegetables and remaining ingredients in stockpot. Simmer until cabbage is tender. Serve with Parmesan cheese. Yield: 6 servings.

Approx Per Serving:
Cal 218; Prot 15 g; Carbo 23 g; T Fat 8 g; Chol 26 mg; Potas 570 mg; Sod 858 mg.

Susan Teal, North Carolina

Lentil Soup

6 slices bacon, chopped

1 cup dried lentils

3 cups frozen mixed vegetables

1 medium potato, peeled, shredded

3 tablespoons tomato paste

6 cups water

Salt and pepper to taste

Brown bacon in uncovered pressure cooker over medium heat until crisp. Add remaining ingredients; mix well. Pressurize and process according to manufacturer's instructions for 25 minutes. Turn off heat. Let stand until depressurized. Yield: 8 servings.

Approx Per Serving:
Cal 181; Prot 11 g; Carbo 30 g; T Fat 3 g; Chol 4 mg; Potas 518 mg; Sod 108 mg.

Merita Fykes, Virginia

Taco Soup

1½ pounds ground beef

1 medium onion, chopped

1   29-ounce can tomatoes

1   16-ounce can kidney beans, drained

1   16-ounce can corn, drained

1   8-ounce can tomato sauce

1 envelope taco seasoning mix

Brown ground beef with onion in saucepan, stirring frequently; drain. Add remaining ingredients. Simmer for 30 minutes.
Yield: 10 servings.

Approx Per Serving:
Cal 278; Prot 18 g; Carbo 29 g; T Fat 11 g; Chol 44 mg; Potas 681 mg; Sod 1410 mg.

Ann Reed, Colorado

Hearty Vegetable Soup

2   12-ounce cans vegetable juice cocktail

2 tablespoons instant beef bouillon

1 small head cabbage, chopped

1 medium onion, sliced

3 small carrots, sliced

½ cup chopped celery

2 cups water

Combine all ingredients in large saucepan. Simmer, covered, for 45 minutes or until vegetables are tender. Yield: 8 servings.

Approx Per Serving:
Cal 44; Prot 2 g; Carbo 10 g; T Fat 0 g; Chol 0 mg; Potas 392 mg; Sod 345 mg.

Esther Walters, Wyoming

CARAMEL APPLE SALAD

1 small package butterscotch
instant pudding mix

8 ounces whipped topping

1 8-ounce can crushed
pineapple

1 cup miniature marshmallows

3 cups chopped unpeeled
apples

1 cup chopped pecans

Combine pudding mix, whipped topping and pineapple in bowl; mix well. Stir in marshmallows, apples and pecans. Chill until serving time. Yield: 8 servings.

Approx Per Serving:
Cal 290; Prot 2 g; Carbo 35 g; T Fat 18 g;
Chol 0 mg; Potas 142 mg; Sod 85 mg.

JoAnn den Broeder, Michigan

DELUXE FRUIT SALAD

1 8-ounce can mandarin
oranges

1 8-ounce can pineapple
chunks

1 4-ounce jar maraschino
cherries

2 apples, chopped

2 bananas, sliced

1 21-ounce can peach
pie filling

1/2 cup chopped pecans

Drain oranges, pineapple and cherries. Combine with apples, bananas, pie filling and pecans in bowl; mix well. Chill until serving time. Yield: 6 servings.

Approx Per Serving:
Cal 297; Prot 2 g; Carbo 62 g; T Fat 7 g;
Chol 0 mg; Potas 413 mg; Sod 33 mg.

Linda Sides, Texas

HEALTHY FRUIT SALAD

2 pints fresh strawberries,
cut into halves

3 cups chopped fresh pineapple

4 bananas, sliced

1 pound seedless grapes,
cut into halves

4 containers low-fat
strawberry yogurt

1 cup chopped pecans

Alternate layers of strawberries, pineapple, bananas and grapes in large bowl until all fruits are used. Spread with yogurt. Sprinkle pecans on top. Chill until serving time. Toss gently at serving time. Yield: 10 servings.

Approx Per Serving:
Cal 255; Prot 5 g; Carbo 42 g; T Fat 10 g;
Chol 3 mg; Potas 545 mg; Sod 40 mg.

Margie Akelewicz, Florida

MIXED FRUIT SALAD

1 cup mandarin orange sections

1 cup pineapple chunks

1 cup banana slices

1 cup seedless grape halves

1 cup coconut

1 cup plain yogurt

Mix fruits and coconut in 2½-quart bowl. Fold in yogurt gently. Chill for 30 minutes or longer. Serve on lettuce-lined serving plates. Yield: 6 servings.

Approx Per Serving:
Cal 182; Prot 3 g; Carbo 34 g; T Fat 5 g; Chol 2 mg; Potas 355 mg; Sod 33 mg.

Georgia Ann Jones, Arkansas

PANTRY SHELF FRUIT SALAD

1   16-ounce can sliced peaches, drained

1   15-ounce can pineapple chunks, drained

1   11-ounce can mandarin oranges, drained

1 cup maraschino cherries

1   21-ounce can apricot pie filling

Combine peaches, pineapple, oranges, cherries and pie filling in bowl. Toss gently to mix well. Chill until serving time. Yield: 8 servings.

Approx Per Serving:
Cal 186; Prot 1 g; Carbo 49 g; T Fat 0 g; Chol 0 mg; Potas 236 mg; Sod 28 mg.

Beth Mitchell, Texas

FRUITED PUDDING SALAD

1 small package vanilla instant pudding mix

1   15-ounce can crushed pineapple

1   8-ounce can mandarin oranges, drained

12 ounces whipped topping

3 bananas, sliced

2 cups miniature marshmallows

Combine dry pudding mix with undrained pineapple in bowl; mix well. Add oranges, whipped topping, bananas, and marshmallows. Chill until serving time. Yield: 10 servings.

Approx Per Serving:
Cal 254; Prot 1 g; Carbo 45 g; T Fat 9 g; Chol 0 mg; Potas 205 mg; Sod 78 mg.

Pam Van Buskirk, Missouri

FRUIT SALAD ROYALE

2 16-ounce cans chunky fruit,
    drained

8 ounces whipped topping

2 cups miniature marshmallows

1 cup chopped pecans

Combine chunky fruit, whipped topping and marshmallows in bowl; mix gently. Sprinkle with pecans. Chill for 45 minutes or longer. Yield: 10 servings.

Approx Per Serving:
Cal 208; Prot 2 g; Carbo 22 g; T Fat 14 g;
Chol 0 mg; Potas 132 mg; Sod 13 mg.

Rosemary Rios, Texas

PINEAPPLE AND CARROT SALAD

2 carrots, shredded

1/4 cup raisins

1/4 cup pineapple yogurt

1 8-ounce can sliced
    pineapple, drained

Combine carrots, raisins and yogurt in bowl; mix well. Place pineapple slices on lettuce-lined salad plate. Top with carrot mixture. Yield: 4 servings.

Approx Per Serving:
Cal 90; Prot 2 g; Carbo 22 g; T Fat 0 g;
Chol 1 mg; Potas 281 mg; Sod 22 mg.

Rebecca Rogers, Oklahoma

RASPBERRY AND COTTAGE CHEESE SALAD

8 ounces cottage cheese

1 small package raspberry
    gelatin

2 cups fresh raspberries

2 cups whipped topping

Combine cottage cheese and dry gelatin in bowl; mix until gelatin is dissolved. Fold in raspberries and whipped topping. Chill until serving time. Yield: 8 servings.

Approx Per Serving:
Cal 143; Prot 5 g; Carbo 18 g; T Fat 6 g;
Chol 4 mg; Potas 74 mg; Sod 153 mg.

Jeannette Needels, Wyoming

TUTTI-FRUTTI SALAD

1 20-ounce can fruit cocktail, drained

2 cups colored miniature marshmallows

8 ounces cottage cheese

1 cup chopped pecans

8 ounces sour cream

1 8-ounce can crushed pineapple, drained

1 cup coconut

Combine fruit cocktail, marshmallows, cottage cheese, pecans, sour cream, pineapple and coconut in bowl; mix well. Chill until serving time. Garnish with cherries and orange sections. Yield: 10 servings.

Approx Per Serving:
Cal 266; Prot 5 g; Carbo 28 g; T Fat 16 g;
Chol 13 mg; Potas 199 mg; Sod 119 mg.

John C. Waldrum, Texas

CHEF'S SALAD

4 cups torn salad greens

4 ounces Swiss cheese, chopped

4 ounces ham, chopped

4 ounces cooked turkey, chopped

1 tomato, cut into wedges

4 hard-boiled eggs, cut into quarters

Place salad greens in bowl. Layer cheese, ham and turkey over greens. Arrange tomato wedges and egg quarters on top. Garnish with black olives. Serve with French or sour cream dressing. Yield: 4 servings.

Approx Per Serving:
Cal 315; Prot 28 g; Carbo 4 g; T Fat 20 g;
Chol 335 mg; Potas 414 mg; Sod 558 mg.

Patty Samples, Missouri

CHEF'S PASTA SALAD

1 16-ounce package vegetable rotini, cooked

2 cups Italian salad dressing

2 cups mayonnaise

1 medium red onion, chopped

4 cups chopped cooked chicken

1 green bell pepper, chopped

Place pasta in large bowl. Mix salad dressing and mayonnaise in small bowl. Add to pasta; mix well. Add onion, chicken and green bell pepper; mix lightly. Garnish with chopped tomato, cucumber and Parmesan cheese. Yield: 12 servings.

Approx Per Serving:
Cal 685; Prot 20 g; Carbo 33 g; T Fat 58 g;
Chol 63 mg; Potas 343 mg; Sod 454 mg.

Maxine McCreary, Kentucky

SALADS

MANDARIN HAM SALAD

3 cups chopped cooked ham

1 16-ounce can pineapple chunks, drained

1 11-ounce can mandarin oranges, drained

1 cup sour cream

1/3 cup mayonnaise

2 cups cold cooked rice

Combine ham, pineapple and oranges in bowl. Combine remaining ingredients in small bowl; mix well. Add to ham mixture; toss lightly. Serve on lettuce-lined plates. Garnish with toasted coconut or slivered almonds. May add canned Bing cherries and 1 1/2 cups miniature marshmallows for a sweeter salad. Yield: 6 servings.

Approx Per Serving:
Cal 450; Prot 12 g; Carbo 37 g; T Fat 29 g; Chol 51 mg; Potas 361 mg; Sod 868 mg.

Mary Franklin, Alabama

WHITE BEAN AND TUNA SALAD

1 6-ounce package radishes, thinly sliced

1/2 teaspoon salt

1 16-ounce can white kidney beans, drained

1 6-ounce can tuna, drained

1 large green onion, chopped

3 tablespoons lemon juice

2 tablespoons oil

1 teaspoon sugar

Combine radishes and 1/2 teaspoon salt in bowl. Let stand for 30 minutes; drain. Add beans, tuna, green onion, lemon juice, oil and sugar; mix well. Chill, covered, in refrigerator. Serve on lettuce-lined plates. Garnish with lemon wedges. Yield: 4 servings.

Approx Per Serving:
Cal 253; Prot 19 g; Carbo 21 g; T Fat 11 g; Chol 7 mg; Potas 524 mg; Sod 822 mg.

Serena Mack, Maryland

SHRIMP AND SPINACH SALAD

2 bunches green onions

1 1/2 pounds fresh spinach, shredded

1 6-ounce can shrimp, drained

1/4 cup soy sauce

1/4 cup oil

Pepper to taste

Cut 3 inches from green onions; mince tops. Layer spinach, onion tops and shrimp on salad plates. Arrange green onions spoke fashion on top. Drizzle with mixture of soy sauce, oil and pepper. Yield: 6 servings.

Approx Per Serving:
Cal 163; Prot 12 g; Carbo 9 g; T Fat 10 g; Chol 49 mg; Potas 884 mg; Sod 826 mg.

Gayle Smith, Florida

Recipes for this photograph are on pages 19, 134 and 141.

QUICK-START BREAKFASTS

A good breakfast makes the day go better.

Easy Baked Apples, 112

Skillet Quiche, 60

Oatmeal Muffins, 102

Milk

Gingerbread Pancakes, 105
or
Orange French Toast, 106

Crisp-Fried Bacon

Banana Shake, 21

LINGUINE SALAD

1 pound linguine

2 cucumbers, seeded, chopped

2 tomatoes, seeded, chopped

1 tablespoon Salad Supreme
spice mix

1   16-ounce bottle of Italian
salad dressing

Break linguine into 2-inch pieces. Cook using package directions; drain. Combine with cucumbers, tomatoes and spice mix in bowl. Add salad dressing; mix well. Chill until serving time. Yield: 10 servings.

Approx Per Serving:
Cal 392; Prot 7 g; Carbo 42 g; T Fat 28 g;
Chol 0 mg; Potas 247 mg; Sod 226 mg.
Nutritional information does not include
Salad Supreme spice mix.

Fran Filek, West Virginia

MACARONI SALAD

2 cups elbow macaroni, cooked

1 cup cubed Cheddar cheese

1 cup sliced celery

1/2 cup chopped green pepper

1/4 cup chopped sweet pickle

1 cup mayonnaise

2 teaspoons prepared mustard

Salt and pepper to taste

Combine macaroni with cheese, celery, green pepper and pickle in bowl. Add mayonnaise, mustard and seasonings; mix well. Chill until serving time. Yield: 6 servings.

Approx Per Serving:
Cal 637; Prot 15 g; Carbo 63 g; T Fat 37 g;
Chol 42 mg; Potas 292 mg; Sod 434 mg.

Betsy Fargo, Illinois

BROCCOLI AND BEAN SALAD

Flowerets of 1 bunch broccoli

1   16-ounce can kidney beans,
drained

1 red onion, chopped

1 cup shredded sharp
Cheddar cheese

1   8-ounce bottle of zesty
Italian salad dressing

Combine broccoli, beans, onion and cheese in bowl. Add salad dressing; mix well. Chill for 6 hours or longer, stirring occasionally. Yield: 8 servings.

Approx Per Serving:
Cal 254; Prot 8 g; Carbo 15 g; T Fat 22 g;
Chol 15 mg; Potas 338 mg; Sod 436 mg.

Peggy Warren, Texas

GOLDEN GARDEN RICE SALAD

1/4 cup olive oil
3 tablespoons white wine vinegar
2 teaspoons Dijon mustard
2 cups broccoli flowerets, blanched
1 1/2 cups sliced mushrooms
4 cups cooked rice
3/4 cup golden raisins
1/4 cup sliced green onions
1/4 cup chopped cilantro

Combine olive oil, vinegar and mustard in bowl; blend with wire whisk. Add broccoli, mushrooms, rice, raisins, green onions and cilantro; toss to coat well. Chill until serving time. Yield: 6 servings.

Photograph for this recipe is on page 69.

CONFETTI SLAW

3 cups shredded red cabbage
1 avocado, finely chopped
1 cup green grape halves
Dry mustard, onion juice and salt to taste
1/3 cup vinegar
1/2 cup oil
1 1/2 tablespoons poppy seed

Combine cabbage, avocado and grape halves in bowl. Combine seasonings, vinegar, oil and poppy seed in jar; shake to mix well. Pour over cabbage mixture. Chill until serving time. Yield: 6 servings.

Approx Per Serving:
Cal 243; Prot 1 g; Carbo 10 g; T Fat 24 g;
Chol 0 mg; Potas 350 mg; Sod 10 mg.

Candy Overton, Texas

FRUITY SLAW

2 cups shredded cabbage
1/4 cup drained crushed pineapple
1/4 cup shredded carrot
1/4 cup raisins
1/4 cup chopped walnuts
1/2 cup mayonnaise

Combine cabbage, pineapple, carrot, raisins and walnuts in bowl. Add mayonnaise; mix well. Chill for 1 hour or longer. Serve on lettuce leaves. Yield: 4 servings.

Approx Per Serving:
Cal 295; Prot 2 g; Carbo 15 g; T Fat 27 g;
Chol 16 mg; Potas 250 mg; Sod 167 mg.

Olive Brown, Ohio

CUCUMBER DELIGHT

3 cucumbers, peeled,
thinly sliced

1 medium onion, sliced
into rings

1 cup sour cream

1/4 cup vinegar

Garlic powder, salt and
pepper to taste

Combine cucumbers and onion in bowl. Mix sour cream, vinegar and seasonings in small bowl. Pour over cucumbers and onion; mix lightly. Let stand for 1 hour before serving. Yield: 6 servings.

Approx Per Serving:
Cal 108; Prot 2 g; Carbo 8 g; T Fat 8 g;
Chol 17 mg; Potas 319 mg; Sod 24 mg.

Michelle Mote, Oklahoma

GREEN BEAN SALAD

1 16-ounce can green beans,
drained

1 tomato, chopped

1 red onion, chopped

1/3 cup Italian salad dressing

Salt and pepper to taste

Combine beans, tomato and onion in bowl. Add salad dressing and seasonings; mix well. Chill for 1 hour or longer. Yield: 4 servings.

Approx Per Serving:
Cal 132; Prot 2 g; Carbo 11 g; T Fat 12 g;
Chol 0 mg; Potas 252 mg; Sod 383 mg.

Rhonda Rostockyj, Texas

MUSHROOM SALAD

8 ounces mushrooms, sliced

2 tomatoes, sliced

1 red onion, sliced

1/2 cup sliced black olives

1/3 cup oil

1/2 cup chopped parsley

1 tablespoon lemon juice

1 tablespoon wine vinegar

Basil, garlic powder, seasoned
salt and pepper to taste

Layer mushrooms, tomatoes, onion and olives in salad bowl. Mix oil, parsley, lemon juice, vinegar and seasonings in bowl. Pour over vegetables. Marinate in refrigerator for 1 hour or longer. Yield: 4 servings.

Approx Per Serving:
Cal 203; Prot 2 g; Carbo 9 g; T Fat 19 g;
Chol 0 mg; Potas 449 mg; Sod 12 mg.

Carol Toomey, Iowa

FRESH TOMATO SALAD

1/2 cup sour cream

Onion salt and garlic salt
to taste

2 medium tomatoes,
thinly sliced

1 red onion, thinly sliced

1 small cucumber, sliced

Combine sour cream and seasonings in bowl; mix well. Alternate layers of tomatoes, onion and cucumber on lettuce-lined serving plate. Spoon dressing over layers. Yield: 4 servings.

Approx Per Serving:
Cal 97; Prot 2 g; Carbo 9 g; T Fat 6 g;
Chol 13 mg; Potas 343 mg; Sod 23 mg.

Diane Spitzer, Illinois

FIESTA TOSSED SALAD

1 large head lettuce, torn

1   12-ounce can white whole
kernel corn, drained

1/2 cup Parmesan cheese

1 cup cherry tomato halves

1   3-ounce can French-fried
onions

3/4 cup creamy garlic
salad dressing

Combine lettuce, corn, cheese, tomatoes and onions in salad bowl. Add salad dressing; toss to mix well. Yield: 6 servings.

Approx Per Serving:
Cal 252; Prot 6 g; Carbo 23 g; T Fat 17 g;
Chol 18 mg; Potas 251 mg; Sod 505 mg.

Julie Haldeman, Ohio

MARINATED VEGETABLE SALAD

3/4 cup vinegar

1/2 cup sugar

1/3 cup corn oil

Salt and pepper to taste

1   16-ounce can tiny green peas

1   16-ounce can French-style
green beans

1   16-ounce can Shoe Peg corn

1 cup chopped celery

Combine vinegar, sugar, corn oil and seasonings in saucepan. Cook until sugar is dissolved, stirring constantly; cool. Drain canned vegetables. Combine with celery in bowl. Pour dressing over vegetables. Chill overnight. May add chopped green bell pepper and green onions if desired. Yield: 12 servings.

Approx Per Serving:
Cal 152; Prot 3 g; Carbo 23 g; T Fat 7 g;
Chol 0 mg; Potas 208 mg; Sod 274 mg.

Karla Riskind, Texas

STROGANOFF BEEFBURGERS

1½ pounds ground beef

3 slices bacon, chopped

½ cup chopped onion

1½ tablespoons flour

¾ teaspoon salt

Pepper to taste

1 can cream of mushroom soup

1 cup sour cream

10 hamburger buns

Brown ground beef with bacon and onion in skillet, stirring frequently; drain. Add flour and seasonings; mix well. Stir in soup. Simmer for 20 minutes, stirring occasionally. Add sour cream; mix well. Heat to serving temperature; do not boil. Serve on toasted buns.
Yield: 10 servings.

Approx Per Serving:
Cal 339; Prot 17 g; Carbo 34 g; T Fat 16 g;
Chol 36 mg; Potas 161 mg; Sod 760 mg.

Christy Fillmore, Maine

SUPER HERO

1   16-ounce loaf French or
Italian bread

½ cup creamy bell pepper or
Italian salad dressing

4   1-ounce slices cooked
turkey breast

4   1-ounce slices corned beef

4   1-ounce slices American
cheese, cut into halves

4 tomato slices, cut into halves

Slice bread into 16 slices, cutting to but not through bottom of loaf. Prepare loaf as for 8 sandwiches with salad dressing, turkey or corned beef, cheese and tomato between every pair of slices, beginning with first 2 slices. Wrap in foil. Bake at 350 degrees for 30 minutes or until heated through. Separate sandwiches to serve. Yield: 8 servings.

Approx Per Serving:
Cal 339; Prot 17 g; Carbo 34 g; T Fat 16 g;
Chol 36 mg; Potas 161 mg; Sod 760 mg.

Jerri Lynn, Oklahoma

PIZZA DOGS

1 pound ground beef

¼ cup chopped onion

⅔ cup tomato sauce

1 cup chopped American cheese

Garlic salt to taste

8 hot dog buns

Brown ground beef with onion in skillet, stirring frequently; drain. Add tomato sauce, cheese and seasoning; mix well. Spoon onto buns. Wrap in foil. Bake at 350 degrees for 20 minutes or until heated through.
Yield: 8 servings.

Approx Per Serving:
Cal 291; Prot 17 g; Carbo 22 g; T Fat 15 g;
Chol 51 mg; Potas 290 mg; Sod 598 mg.

Lois Hardison, West Virginia

Taco Crescents

3/4 **pound ground beef**

1 **onion, minced**

1 **envelope taco seasoning mix**

1 **3-ounce can ripe olives, chopped**

2 **eggs, beaten**

2 **8-count cans refrigerater crescent rolls**

3/4 **cup shredded Cheddar cheese**

Brown ground beef with onion in skillet, stirring frequently; drain. Stir in seasoning mix and olives; cool. Add eggs; mix well. Unroll and separate roll dough. Spoon 1 1/2 tablespoons ground beef mixture onto each triangle. Roll to enclose filling; shape into crescents. Place on baking sheet. Top with cheese. Bake at 375 degrees for 15 minutes. Serve with salsa. Yield: 16 servings.

Approx Per Serving:
Cal 210; Prot 8 g; Carbo 17 g; T Fat 12 g; Chol 54 mg; Potas 172 mg; Sod 848 mg.

Ida Weber, Florida

Egg Salad with Bacon and Cheese

6 **slices crisp-fried bacon, crumbled**

6 **hard-boiled eggs, finely chopped**

8 **ounces Swiss cheese, shredded**

1/4 **cup candied dill pickle**

3/4 **cup mayonnaise**

2 1/2 **teaspoons mustard**

Salt and seasoned pepper to taste

16 **slices multi-grain sandwich bread**

Combine bacon, eggs and cheese in bowl; mix well. Add pickle, mayonnaise, mustard and seasonings; mix well. Spread between bread slices. Yield: 8 servings.

Approx Per Serving:
Cal 473; Prot 19 g; Carbo 27 g; T Fat 33 g; Chol 248 mg; Potas 194 mg; Sod 632 mg.

Betty Ann Cross, Illinois

Fried Ham Sandwiches

2 **cups ground baked ham**

1/2 **cup soft bread crumbs**

1/4 **cup chopped green onion**

1/3 **cup milk**

1 **tablespoon shortening**

1 **cup sour cream**

6 **hamburger buns**

Combine first 4 ingredients in bowl; mix well. Shape into patties. Brown on both sides in shortening in skillet. Remove ham patties. Blend sour cream into pan drippings. Cook until warm; do not boil. Place ham patties on buns. Spoon sour cream sauce over top. Yield: 6 servings.

Approx Per Serving:
Cal 363; Prot 16 g; Carbo 27 g; T Fat 21 g; Chol 48 mg; Potas 284 mg; Sod 870 mg.

Aileen Parker, Mississippi

GIANT HAM SANDWICH

1 cup margarine, softened

3 tablespoons poppy seed

1 tablespoon Worcestershire sauce

3 tablespoons Dijon-style mustard

1 large round loaf French bread

8 ounces baked ham, thinly sliced

8 ounces Swiss cheese, thinly sliced

Combine first 4 ingredients in bowl; mix well. Slice top half from loaf. Spread cut sides with margarine mixture. Layer ham and cheese on bottom half; replace top. Wrap in foil. Bake at 400 degrees for 15 minutes or until cheese melts. Cool slightly. Cut into wedges.
Yield: 8 servings.

Approx Per Serving:
Cal 486; Prot 18 g; Carbo 20 g; T Fat 37 g;
Chol 43 mg; Potas 179 mg; Sod 972 mg.

Angela Hughes, South Carolina

MICROWAVE CHILI AND CHICKEN BURRITOS

2 cups chopped cooked chicken

2 tablespoons chopped green chilies

2 tablespoons chopped onion

1 cup shredded Monterey Jack cheese

2 tablespoons sour cream

6 flour tortillas

Combine first 5 ingredients in bowl; mix well. Spoon onto tortillas; roll to enclose filling. Wrap each in paper towel. Microwave on High for 30 to 45 seconds each or until cheese melts. Let stand for 1 minute before serving.
Yield: 6 servings.

Approx Per Serving:
Cal 277; Prot 21 g; Carbo 20 g; T Fat 13 g;
Chol 61 mg; Potas 186 mg; Sod 278 mg.

Mattie Joyner, Wyoming

HOT BROWN

12 slices crisp-fried bacon

12 1-ounce slices cooked chicken breast

12 slices tomato

6 English muffins, split

2 cups cheese sauce

Layer 2 slices bacon, 1 slice chicken and 1 slice tomato on each muffin half. Heat cheese sauce in saucepan until bubbly. Spoon over tomato.
Yield: 6 servings.

Approx Per Serving:
Cal 466; Prot 33 g; Carbo 33 g; T Fat 21 g;
Chol 84 mg; Potas 741 mg; Sod 988 mg.

Carla Schroer, California

Grilled Kielbasa Sandwiches

2 pounds kielbasa	Cut kielbasa into 3-inch portions. Split lengthwise; do not cut through. Place on grill over hot coals. Sprinkle with lemon juice and oregano. Grill until brown, turning frequently. Serve on rolls. Yield: 4 servings.
Juice of 2 lemons	
Oregano to taste	
4 sandwich rolls, split	

Approx Per Serving:
Cal 556; Prot 21 g; Carbo 40 g; T Fat 35 g;
Chol 74 mg; Potas 384 mg; Sod 1563 mg.

Billie Reasonover, Virginia

Chef Salad Sandwich

1 16-ounce round loaf French bread	Slice bread into 3 layers. Spread cut sides with salad dressing. Layer spinach, ham, onion and Monterey Jack cheese on bottom layer; cover with center bread slice. Layer with turkey breast, tomato and Colby cheese; replace top of loaf. Cut into wedges. Yield: 6 servings.
3/4 cup creamy Italian salad dressing	
2 cups spinach leaves	
8 ounces baked ham, thinly sliced	
1/2 small onion, thinly sliced	
4 ounces Monterey Jack cheese, sliced	
8 ounces cooked turkey breast, thinly sliced	
1 tomato, sliced	
4 ounces Colby cheese, sliced	

Approx Per Serving:
Cal 662; Prot 37 g; Carbo 44 g; T Fat 40 g;
Chol 85 mg; Potas 503 mg; Sod 1286 mg.

Alethea Wood, West Virginia

Tunaburgers

1 7-ounce can tuna, drained	Combine first 5 ingredients in bowl; mix well. Butter bread slices. Spread with tuna mixture. Place on baking sheet. Bake at 350 degrees for 15 minutes. Yield: 4 servings.
1 cup chopped celery	
1/2 cup shredded mozzarella cheese	
1 small onion, minced	
1/4 cup mayonnaise	
1/4 cup butter, softened	
4 slices bread	

Approx Per Serving:
Cal 428; Prot 20 g; Carbo 18 g; T Fat 31 g;
Chol 59 mg; Potas 284 mg; Sod 575 mg.

Kathy Purcell, Michigan

Magical Main Dishes

BEEF TIPS WITH RICE

2 pounds lean beef chuck cubes

1 envelope dry onion soup mix

1 can cream of mushroom soup

1 cup ginger ale

3 cups hot cooked rice

Layer beef, soup mix and soup in Crock•Pot. Pour ginger ale over top. Cook on Low for 6 to 8 hours. Serve over rice. May bake in tightly covered casserole at 275 degrees for 4 hours. Yield: 6 servings.

Approx Per Serving:
Cal 455; Prot 35 g; Carbo 33 g; T Fat 20 g; Chol 108 mg; Potas 337 mg; Sod 590 mg.

Jenny Halloran, Tennessee

BEEF KABOBS

1½ pounds round steak

2 green bell peppers, cut into squares

1 pound fresh mushrooms

½ cup spicy brown mustard

¼ cup oil

2 tablespoons soy sauce

2 teaspoons lemon juice

Cut steak into 1½-inch cubes. Thread steak cubes, green pepper squares and mushrooms alternately onto skewers. Place on rack in broiler pan. Blend mustard, oil, soy sauce and lemon juice in small bowl. Brush over steak and vegetables. Broil 4 to 5 inches from heat source until steak is cooked to desired degree of doneness, basting frequently with mustard mixture. Yield: 6 servings.

Approx Per Serving:
Cal 275; Prot 24 g; Carbo 7 g; T Fat 17 g; Chol 64 mg; Potas 592 mg; Sod 643 mg.

Kaylie Brandshaw, California

GIANT PASTIES

2 frozen pie shells, thawed

4 potatoes, peeled, chopped

1 onion, chopped

1 cup chopped rutabaga

1 pound round steak, chopped

¼ cup butter

Salt and pepper to taste

Place pie shells on lightly floured surface. Layer half the potatoes, onion, rutabaga and steak on half of each pie shell. Dot with butter; sprinkle with salt and pepper. Fold pie shells over to enclose filling; seal edges. Place on baking sheet. Bake at 400 degrees for 45 minutes or until golden brown. Cut into wedges. May prepare smaller size pasties to serve cold as sandwiches. Yield: 6 servings.

Approx Per Serving:
Cal 631; Prot 22 g; Carbo 64 g; T Fat 32 g; Chol 63 mg; Potas 852 mg; Sod 470 mg.

Joanna Rudd, Michigan

CROCK•POT ROAST

1   4-pound beef rump roast
4 large potatoes, peeled, quartered
8 baby carrots
1 onion, sliced
1 envelope dry onion soup mix
1 can cream of mushroom soup

Trim fat from roast. Place potatoes, carrots and onions in Crock•Pot. Place roast on vegetables. Sprinkle with soup mix; top with soup. Cook on Low for 6 to 8 hours. Yield: 8 servings.

Approx Per Serving:
Cal 465; Prot 46 g; Carbo 33 g; T Fat 16 g; Chol 128 mg; Potas 969 mg; Sod 472 mg.

Judy Peterson, Connecticut

GRILLED FLANK STEAK

1½ pounds flank steak
Garlic powder to taste
¼ cup soy sauce
2 tablespoons Worcestershire sauce
2 tablespoons oil

Sprinkle steak with garlic powder; prick with fork. Place in shallow pan. Pour mixture of soy sauce, Worcestershire sauce and oil over steak. Marinate in refrigerator for several hours, turning occasionally. Drain, reserving marinade. Place in oven on rack in broiler pan or on grill over medium coals. Broil or grill for 7 to 9 minutes on each side or to desired degree of doneness, brushing frequently with reserved marinade. Slice thinly cross grain.
Yield: 4 servings.

Approx Per Serving:
Cal 298; Prot 33 g; Carbo 3 g; T Fat 17 g; Chol 96 mg; Potas 401 mg; Sod 1154 mg.

Grace Kathcart, Tennessee

COUNTRY-STYLE STEAK-IN-THE-POT

1 pound round steak, tenderized
½ cup flour
¼ cup shortening
¼ cup chopped onion
1 can cream of mushroom soup
1 cup water

Cut steak into serving portions. Coat with flour. Brown on both sides in shortening in skillet. Place in Crock•Pot. Sprinkle onion over steak. Add soup and water to pan drippings in skillet; mix well. Pour over steak. Cook on Low for 6 hours or until steak is tender. Yield: 4 servings.

Approx Per Serving:
Cal 400; Prot 24 g; Carbo 18 g; T Fat 25 g; Chol 65 mg; Potas 287 mg; Sod 652 mg.

Sandra Honeycutt, North Carolina

SWISS STEAK

2 pounds round steak

3/4 cup flour

3 tablespoons oil

Salt and pepper to taste

1 16-ounce can tomatoes

1 can cream of mushroom soup

1 can onion soup

1 1/2 teaspoons Worcestershire sauce

Cut steak into serving portions. Coat with flour. Brown on both sides in oil in skillet. Place in shallow baking pan. Add salt and pepper, tomatoes, soups and Worcestershire sauce. Bake, covered, with foil, at 275 degrees for 4 hours or until tender. May cook in Crock•Pot on Low for 6 hours. May add chopped fresh tomatoes, green bell pepper or onion. Serve over hot cooked rice or noodles.
Yield: 6 servings.

Approx Per Serving:
Cal 395; Prot 32 g; Carbo 21 g; T Fat 20 g; Chol 86 mg; Potas 515 mg; Sod 815 mg.

Pat French, Oklahoma

STEAK AND ZUCCHINI SUPPER

1 pound round steak

1 tablespoon oil

1 10-ounce can mushroom gravy

1/2 envelope spaghetti sauce mix

1/2 cup water

3 medium zucchini, sliced

Cut steak into thin strips. Stir-fry in hot oil in skillet. Add gravy, sauce mix and water; mix well. Cook, covered, over low heat for 20 minutes, stirring occasionally. Add zucchini. Cook for 10 minutes or until zucchini is tender-crisp, stirring occasionally. Serve over hot cooked rice or noodles. Yield: 4 servings.

Approx Per Serving:
Cal 228; Prot 23 g; Carbo 7 g; T Fat 12 g; Chol 64 mg; Potas 453 mg; Sod 546 mg.

Montelle Diego, California

LAZY STEW

1 pound round steak

1 16-ounce can potatoes

1 16-ounce can whole kernel corn

1 4-ounce can mushrooms

Salt and pepper to taste

1 can cream of mushroom soup

Cut steak into bite-sized pieces; place in Crock•Pot. Drain vegetables, reserving liquid. Add vegetables and seasonings to Crock•Pot. Pour soup and 1/2 soup can reserved vegetable liquid over top. Cook on Low for 6 hours or longer. Yield: 4 servings.

Approx Per Serving:
Cal 393; Prot 28 g; Carbo 44 g; T Fat 14 g; Chol 65 mg; Potas 727 mg; Sod 1265 mg.

Clair Patterson, Wisconsin

MICROWAVE QUICK STROGANOFF

1 clove of garlic, crushed
2 tablespoons butter
1 pound round steak, cut into strips
1/2 cup thinly sliced onion
1 can cream of mushroom soup
3/4 cup sour cream
1 tablespoon tomato paste

Microwave garlic and butter in 2-quart glass baking dish on High for 1 to 2 minutes. Add steak and onion. Microwave, covered, on High for 3 minutes or until steak is no longer pink. Stir in soup, sour cream and tomato paste. Microwave for 7 to 9 minutes or until steak is tender, stirring occasionally. Let stand for 2 minutes. Serve over hot cooked noodles. Yield: 4 servings.

Approx Per Serving:
Cal 381; Prot 24 g; Carbo 10 g; T Fat 27 g; Chol 99 mg; Potas 393 mg; Sod 726 mg.

Martha Plunkett, Arkansas

MACARONI AND CORNED BEEF CASSEROLE

1 7-ounce package macaroni and cheese dinner
1 tablespoon butter
2 1/2 cups boiling water
2 cups chopped corned beef

Combine uncooked macaroni and cheese sauce powder in 3-quart casserole. Add butter and boiling water; mix well. Stir in corned beef. Bake, covered, at 375 degrees for 25 minutes or until macaroni is tender. Yield: 4 servings.

Approx Per Serving:
Cal 351; Prot 24 g; Carbo 35 g; T Fat 13 g; Chol 57 mg; Potas 78 mg; Sod 999 mg.

Charlene Boone, Colorado

CORNED BEEF PIZZA

2 cups sifted flour
2 teaspoons baking powder
2/3 cup Thousand Island salad dressing
1/3 cup milk
1 12-ounce can corned beef, flaked
1 cup shredded Cheddar cheese
3/4 cup sour cream
1/2 teaspoon dry mustard

Mix flour and baking powder in bowl. Add salad dressing and milk; mix until mixture forms ball. Press into 14-inch pizza pan. Sprinkle with corned beef. Mix cheese, sour cream and dry mustard in bowl. Spread over corned beef. Bake at 425 degrees for 20 minutes or until golden brown. Yield: 6 servings.

Approx Per Serving:
Cal 545; Prot 26 g; Carbo 38 g; T Fat 31 g; Chol 90 mg; Potas 228 mg; Sod 1011 mg.

Judy Hancock, West Virginia

GIANT STUFFED BURGER

1 egg, beaten

1¼ cups crushed
herb-seasoned stuffing mix

1　4-ounce can chopped
mushrooms, drained

⅓ cup beef broth

¼ cup sliced green onions

2 tablespoons melted butter

2 pounds ground beef

Salt and pepper to taste

Combine egg, stuffing mix, mushrooms, beef broth, green onions and butter in bowl; mix well. Mix ground beef with salt and pepper in bowl. Shape into two 8-inch patties on waxed paper. Spoon stuffing mixture onto 1 patty, covering to within 1 inch of edge. Top with remaining patty; seal edges. Place on greased rack over medium coals. Grill for 10 to 12 minutes on each side or to desired degree of doneness. Cut into wedges; serve with warm catsup. Yield: 8 servings.

Approx Per Serving:
Cal 404; Prot 27 g; Carbo 27 g; T Fat 21 g;
Chol 116 mg; Potas 297 mg; Sod 799 mg.

Karen Faith Brown, North Carolina

CONFETTI CASSEROLE

2 pounds ground beef

½ cup chopped onion

2 tablespoons brown sugar

Dry mustard, salt and pepper
to taste

8 ounces cream cheese, chopped

2　8-ounce cans tomato sauce

2　10-ounce packages frozen
mixed vegetables, thawed

Brown ground beef with onion in skillet, stirring until ground beef is crumbly; drain. Stir in brown sugar, seasonings and cream cheese. Cook until cream cheese is melted, stirring constantly. Add tomato sauce and vegetables. Spoon into 9x13-inch baking dish. Bake, covered, at 375 degrees for 40 minutes. Bake, uncovered, for 10 minutes longer. May top with corn chips if desired. Yield: 8 servings.

Approx Per Serving:
Cal 404; Prot 26 g; Carbo 18 g; T Fat 26 g;
Chol 105 mg; Potas 647 mg; Sod 518 mg.

Cathy Brown, Arkansas

MICROWAVE BEEFY MACARONI GOULASH

1 pound ground beef

1 cup macaroni, cooked

1　16-ounce can tomato purée

Salt and pepper to taste

1 tablespoon chopped parsley

Crumble ground beef into 3-quart glass dish. Microwave on High for 4 to 5 minutes or until no longer pink, stirring once; drain. Stir in remaining ingredients. Microwave on High for 8 minutes, stirring once. Microwave, covered, on Low for 4 minutes. Let stand for 5 minutes. Yield: 4 servings.

Approx Per Serving:
Cal 329; Prot 25 g; Carbo 22 g; T Fat 16 g;
Chol 74 mg; Potas 764 mg; Sod 88 mg.

Joanne Laurino, Florida

HUNGRY JACK CASSEROLE

1 pound ground beef

1 16-ounce can pork and beans

1/2 cup barbecue sauce

1 tablespoon sugar

Onion flakes and salt to taste

1 cup shredded Cheddar cheese

1 8-count can flaky
refrigerator biscuits

Brown ground beef in skillet, stirring until crumbly; drain. Stir in next 3 ingredients. Add seasonings. Spoon into 2-quart baking dish. Sprinkle with cheese. Cut biscuits into halves. Place cut side down around edges and over top of casserole. Bake at 350 degrees for 15 minutes or until brown. Yield: 6 servings.

Approx Per Serving:
Cal 422; Prot 25 g; Carbo 33 g; T Fat 21 g;
Chol 76 mg; Potas 451 mg; Sod 916 mg.

Lisa Lyon, Tennessee

TACO SURPRISE

8 ounces ground beef

1 cup buttermilk baking mix

1/4 cup cold water

2 medium tomatoes, thinly
sliced

1/2 cup chopped green
bell pepper

1/2 cup sour cream

1/4 cup mayonnaise

1 cup shredded Cheddar cheese

Brown ground beef in skillet, stirring until crumbly; drain. Combine baking mix and water in bowl; mix well. Press over bottom and sides of greased 8x8-inch baking dish. Layer ground beef, tomatoes and green pepper over dough. Mix remaining ingredients in bowl. Spoon over layers. Bake at 375 degrees for 20 minutes or until light brown. Yield: 6 servings.

Approx Per Serving:
Cal 360; Prot 14 g; Carbo 18 g; T Fat 26 g;
Chol 58 mg; Potas 266 mg; Sod 469 mg.

Tamara Myers, New York

TOSTADO CASSEROLE

1 pound ground beef

1 envelope taco seasoning mix

1 15-ounce can tomato sauce

2 16-ounce cans refried beans

2 1/2 cups corn chips

1/2 cup shredded Cheddar
cheese

Brown ground beef in skillet, stirring until crumbly; drain. Stir in seasoning mix and 1 1/2 cups tomato sauce. Mix remaining tomato sauce and refried beans in bowl. Layer 2 cups corn chips, ground beef mixture and bean mixture in baking dish. Bake at 375 degrees for 25 minutes. Sprinkle with remaining corn chips and cheese. Bake for 5 minutes longer or until cheese is melted. Yield: 6 servings.

Approx Per Serving:
Cal 553; Prot 30 g; Carbo 64 g; T Fat 20 g;
Chol 59 mg; Potas 1224 mg; Sod 4040 mg.

Jeannette A. Smith, West Virginia

BEEF AND NOODLE BAKE

8 ounces noodles, cooked

1 cup cream-style cottage cheese

1 cup sour cream

1 cup sliced green onions

1 pound ground beef

Garlic salt to taste

1 cup tomato sauce

1 cup shredded Cheddar cheese

Combine first 4 ingredients in bowl; mix well. Brown ground beef in skillet, stirring until crumbly; drain. Add garlic salt and tomato sauce. Simmer for 5 minutes. Alternate layers of ground beef and noodles in baking dish until all ingredients are used. Top with Cheddar cheese. Bake at 350 degrees for 30 minutes. Yield: 6 servings.

Approx Per Serving:
Cal 350; Prot 16 g; Carbo 35 g; T Fat 16 g; Chol 74 mg; Potas 380 mg; Sod 527 mg.

Anna B. Bender, Wisconsin

GREEN BEAN AND BURGER CASSEROLE

1 pound lean ground beef

1 cup chopped onion

3 cups cooked rice

1/2 cup shredded Cheddar cheese

Garlic salt and pepper to taste

1   16-ounce can green beans

1 can cream of celery soup

1/4 cup mayonnaise

3 tablespoons chopped pimentos

1/2 cup milk

Brown ground beef with onion in skillet, stirring until ground beef is crumbly; drain. Add rice, cheese and seasonings; mix well. Spoon into greased 9x13-inch baking dish. Top with drained green beans. Mix soup, mayonnaise, pimentos and milk in bowl. Pour over casserole. Bake at 350 degrees for 30 minutes. Yield: 8 servings.

Approx Per Serving:
Cal 333; Prot 16 g; Carbo 27 g; T Fat 18 g; Chol 55 mg; Potas 309 mg; Sod 553 mg.

Rhonda Hayes, Kansas

SPANISH RICE CASSEROLE

1 pound ground beef

1/4 cup chopped onion

1   15-ounce can chili beans

1   15-ounce can Spanish rice

1   8-ounce package corn chips

1 cup shredded Cheddar cheese

Brown ground beef with onion in large skillet, stirring until ground beef is crumbly; drain. Stir in beans and rice. Sprinkle 1/3 of the chips into 9x13-inch baking dish. Layer ground beef mixture, remaining chips and cheese 1/2 at a time in prepared dish. Bake at 350 degrees until bubbly. Yield: 6 servings.

Approx Per Serving:
Cal 572; Prot 27 g; Carbo 50 g; T Fat 29 g; Chol 69 mg; Potas 471 mg; Sod 717 mg.

Connie Perry, Michigan

CHILI CON CARNE

2 pounds ground beef

2 medium onions, chopped

2 8-ounce cans tomato sauce

2 cans tomato soup

2 soup cans water

Chili powder and salt to taste

2 16-ounce cans kidney beans

1 bay leaf

Brown ground beef with onions in saucepan, stirring until ground beef is crumbly; drain. Add tomato sauce, soup and water. Stir in chili powder and salt. Bring to a boil. Add beans and bay leaf. Simmer until serving time. Remove bay leaf. Yield: 8 servings.

Approx Per Serving:
Cal 401; Prot 29 g; Carbo 33 g; T Fat 18 g; Chol 74 mg; Potas 964 mg; Sod 1332 mg.

Ethel Petry, Oklahoma

CROCK•POT CHILI

2 pounds lean ground beef

1 large onion, chopped

1 clove of garlic, minced

3 cans tomato soup

3 16-ounce cans kidney beans

1 tablespoon chili powder

Brown ground beef with onion and garlic in skillet, stirring until ground beef is crumbly; drain. Place in 3½-quart Crock•Pot. Add soup, beans and chili powder; mix well. Cook on Low for 6 to 8 hours, stirring occasionally. Yield: 8 servings.

Approx Per Serving:
Cal 454; Prot 32 g; Carbo 42 g; T Fat 18 g; Chol 74 mg; Potas 966 mg; Sod 1450 mg.

Kathy Wiser, Tennessee

OVEN PORCUPINES

1 pound ground beef

½ cup rice

1 cup chopped onion

Celery salt, garlic powder, salt and pepper to taste

1 15-ounce can tomato sauce

2 teaspoons Worcestershire sauce

1 cup water

Combine ground beef, rice, onion and seasonings in bowl; mix well. Shape by teaspoonfuls into balls. Place in 8-inch baking dish. Mix tomato sauce, Worcestershire sauce and water in bowl. Pour over meatballs. Bake, covered, at 350 degrees for 45 minutes. Bake, uncovered, for 15 minutes longer. Yield: 4 servings.

Approx Per Serving:
Cal 361; Prot 25 g; Carbo 30 g; T Fat 16 g; Chol 74 mg; Potas 753 mg; Sod 734 mg.

Beverly M. Ragsdale, Tennessee

MICROWAVE SWEET AND SOUR MEATBALLS

1 pound ground beef

1 onion, finely chopped

1/2 cup drained crushed pineapple

Salt to taste

1 can tomato soup

1/4 cup packed brown sugar

3 tablespoons lemon juice

Combine ground beef, onion, pineapple and salt in bowl; mix well. Shape into small balls. Combine soup, brown sugar and lemon juice in 8x8-inch glass dish. Microwave on High for 7 minutes, stirring once. Add meatballs. Microwave on Medium for 5 minutes. Spoon sauce over meatballs; rotate dish. Microwave for 5 minutes longer. Serve over rice.
Yield: 6 servings.

Approx Per Serving:
Cal 244; Prot 15 g; Carbo 21 g; T Fat 12 g; Chol 49 mg; Potas 382 mg; Sod 401 mg.

Elizabeth Grubbs, Kentucky

CORNY MEATBALLS

1 pound ground beef

1 onion, grated

1 egg

3/4 cup cracker crumbs

1 7-ounce can sliced water chestnuts, drained

1 10-ounce package frozen corn, thawed

1 tablespoon teriyaki sauce

Salt and pepper to taste

1 can cream of onion soup

Combine ground beef, onion, egg, cracker crumbs, water chestnuts, corn, teriyaki sauce and seasonings in bowl; mix well. Shape into large balls. Place in greased baking dish. Spoon soup over top. Bake, covered, at 425 degrees for 30 minutes. Bake, uncovered, for 15 minutes or until meatballs are cooked through.
Yield: 4 servings.

Approx Per Serving:
Cal 451; Prot 29 g; Carbo 41 g; T Fat 20 g; Chol 148 mg; Potas 566 mg; Sod 1122 mg.

Stephanie Alcorn Siskiyou, California

CHUCK WAGON MEAT LOAF

1 1/2 pounds lean ground beef

6 crackers, crushed

1/2 cup chopped onion

Garlic powder, paprika, salt and pepper to taste

1 1/2 cups Cheddar cheese cubes

2 eggs, slightly beaten

3/4 cup milk

Combine ground beef, cracker crumbs, onion and seasonings in bowl. Add cheese, eggs and milk; mix well. Shape into loaf. Place in greased loaf pan. Bake at 350 degrees for 1 hour or to desired degree of doneness. Yield: 6 servings.

Approx Per Serving:
Cal 406; Prot 31 g; Carbo 5 g; T Fat 29 g; Chol 200 mg; Potas 371 mg; Sod 315 mg.

Lenora Abel, Minnesota

Microwave Meat Loaf

2 pounds ground beef

2 eggs, slightly beaten

1 medium onion, chopped

1/4 cup cracker crumbs

Salt and pepper to taste

1 8-ounce can tomato sauce

1 teaspoon prepared mustard

1/4 cup packed brown sugar

Combine ground beef, eggs, onion, cracker crumbs, seasonings and half the tomato sauce in bowl; mix well. Pack into glass ring mold or around inverted glass in 2-quart glass baking dish. Mix remaining tomato sauce, mustard and brown sugar in bowl. Pour over meat loaf. Microwave, uncovered, on High for 12 to 14 minutes or until cooked through. Let stand for 5 minutes before serving. Yield: 8 servings.

Approx Per Serving:
Cal 302; Prot 23 g; Carbo 12 g; T Fat 18 g;
Chol 143 mg; Potas 437 mg; Sod 299 mg.

Martha Goad, Tennessee

Beef and Potato Pie

1 pound ground round

1 medium onion, chopped

1 8-ounce can tomato sauce

Salt and pepper to taste

3 medium potatoes, peeled, cooked

2 tablespoons margarine

1/2 cup milk

Combine ground round, onion, tomato sauce, salt and pepper in bowl; mix well. Press into 8-inch pie plate. Bake at 425 degrees for 20 to 30 minutes or until brown. Whip potatoes with margarine and milk in bowl until smooth. Spoon into beef crust. Broil until light brown. Yield: 6 servings.

Approx Per Serving:
Cal 253; Prot 17 g; Carbo 19 g; T Fat 12 g;
Chol 51 mg; Potas 570 mg; Sod 310 mg.

Michele Bond, North Carolina

Easy Tamale Pie

1 pound ground beef

1 envelope taco seasoning mix

1 16-ounce can tomatoes

1 16-ounce can cream-style corn

1 small package corn bread mix

Brown ground beef in skillet, stirring until crumbly; drain. Add taco seasoning mix; mix well. Stir in tomatoes and corn. Simmer for 30 minutes. Spoon into baking dish. Prepare corn bread batter using package directions. Pour over ground beef mixture. Bake according to package directions until brown.
Yield: 6 servings.

Approx Per Serving:
Cal 406; Prot 20 g; Carbo 53 g; T Fat 14 g;
Chol 49 mg; Potas 624 mg; Sod 3316 mg.

Barbara Riley, Tennessee

PORK MEDALLIONS WITH LEMON AND PECAN SPINACH

8   2-ounce medallions of pork
      tenderloin

Salt and pepper to taste

1 tablespoon margarine

2 tablespoons lemon juice

1/8 teaspoon hot pepper sauce

1   10-ounce package frozen
      chopped spinach, thawed

2 tablespoons chopped pecans

2 green onions, chopped

Pound pork medallions to 1-inch thickness. Sprinkle with salt and pepper. Brown for 3 to 4 minutes on each side in margarine in heavy skillet over medium-high heat. Remove pork to warm plate. Stir lemon juice and pepper sauce into drippings in skillet. Drain spinach. Stir in pecans, green onions and spinach. Cook over low heat until spinach is tender and heated through. Place on serving plate; arrange pork on top. Garnish with lemon slices and sprigs of parsley. Yield: 4 servings.

Photograph for this recipe is on Cover.

SAUCY APPLE PORK CHOPS

6 thick pork chops

Salt and pepper to taste

1   14-ounce jar spiced apple
      rings

2/3 cup applesauce

1 teaspoon lemon juice

1/3 cup golden raisins

1 tablespoon cornstarch

1/3 cup water

Brown pork chops on both sides in Dutch oven; drain. Sprinkle with salt and pepper. Drain apple rings, reserving liquid. Combine reserved liquid, applesauce and lemon juice in bowl; mix well. Add to pork chops. Stir in raisins. Bake, covered, at 350 degrees for 1 hour. Remove pork chops to hot platter. Stir mixture of cornstarch and water into liquid in Dutch oven. Cook until thickened. Add apple rings. Cook for 1 minute. Serve over pork chops. Yield: 6 servings.

Approx Per Serving:
Cal 360; Prot 37 g; Carbo 25 g; T Fat 12 g;
Chol 112 mg; Potas 608 mg; Sod 92 mg.

Amanda Halpin, South Carolina

BARBECUED PORK CHOPS

6 medium pork chops

3/4 cup barbecue sauce

1 sweet onion, sliced into rings

1 green bell pepper, sliced
      into rings

1/4 teaspoon garlic powder

1/4 cup water

Place trimmed pork chops in baking dish. Pour barbecue sauce over chops. Top with onion and green pepper rings. Sprinkle with garlic powder. Add water to dish. Bake, covered with foil, at 225 degrees for 3 hours. Yield: 6 servings.

Approx Per Serving:
Cal 294; Prot 37 g; Carbo 6 g; T Fat 13 g;
Chol 112 mg; Potas 604 mg; Sod 344 mg.

Becky McCormick, Tennessee

Hawaiian Pork Chops

4 pork chops
2 tablespoons brown sugar
1   8-ounce can crushed pineapple
2 tablespoons tomato sauce
1/3 teaspoon curry powder
Salt and pepper to taste

Brown pork chops on both sides in skillet sprayed with nonstick cooking spray. Place in baking dish. Combine brown sugar, pineapple, tomato sauce and seasonings in bowl; mix well. Spoon over pork chops. Bake at 350 degrees for 1 hour. Yield: 4 servings.

Approx Per Serving:
Cal 333; Prot 37 g; Carbo 19 g; T Fat 12 g; Chol 112 mg; Potas 586 mg; Sod 138 mg.

Chantel DeRuiter, California

Oven-Fried Pork Chops

1 tablespoon margarine
2/3 cup buttermilk baking mix
1 teaspoon paprika
1 1/2 teaspoons seasoned salt
1/4 teaspoon pepper
6 pork chops

Melt margarine in 9x13-inch baking dish. Combine baking mix with paprika, seasoned salt and pepper on waxed paper. Coat pork chops with mixture. Arrange in prepared baking dish. Bake at 425 degrees for 35 minutes. Turn chops over. Bake for 15 minutes longer. Yield: 6 servings.

Approx Per Serving:
Cal 339; Prot 37 g; Carbo 9 g; T Fat 16 g; Chol 112 mg; Potas 497 mg; Sod 820 mg.

Joan G. Bovee, Indiana

Pork Chops with Yams

4 thick pork chops
1   8-ounce can sliced pineapple
2   16-ounce cans yams
Basil, cinnamon, nutmeg, allspice and pepper to taste
1   8-ounce can sliced water chestnuts, drained

Brown pork chops in skillet sprayed with nonstick cooking spray. Remove chops and drain excess pan drippings. Drain pineapple and yams, reserving juices. Add reserved juices and seasonings to skillet, stirring to deglaze. Add pork chops. Cook, covered, over low heat for 45 minutes, basting occasionally. Add yams, pineapple and water chestnuts. Cook, covered, for 15 minutes longer. Yield: 4 servings.

Approx Per Serving:
Cal 538; Prot 41 g; Carbo 66 g; T Fat 12 g; Chol 112 mg; Potas 1309 mg; Sod 213 mg.

Mildred Wilcox, Michigan

Microwave Pork Ribs and Sauerkraut

2 pounds pork ribs
1   16-ounce can sauerkraut, drained
1 cup applesauce
1 small onion, finely chopped
2 tablespoons brown sugar
Caraway seed and garlic powder to taste

Place ribs in glass baking dish. Microwave, loosely covered, on High for 13 to 15 minutes or until no longer pink; drain. Turn ribs over and rearrange in dish. Mix remaining ingredients in bowl. Spoon over ribs. Microwave, loosely covered, on High for 10 to 12 minutes or until tender. Yield: 4 servings.

Approx Per Serving:
Cal 700; Prot 45 g; Carbo 26 g; T Fat 46 g;
Chol 181 mg; Potas 781 mg; Sod 895 mg.

Dixie Spears, Georgia

Festive Ham Casserole

6 medium sweet potatoes
1   28-ounce can peach halves
1 tablespoon brown sugar
6 slices cured ham
1/2 cup cranberry sauce

Cook sweet potatoes in water to cover in saucepan for 15 to 20 minutes or until tender. Drain and cut potatoes into halves. Drain peaches, reserving syrup. Stir brown sugar into reserved syrup. Layer sweet potatoes, peach syrup and ham slices 1/2 at a time in greased baking dish. Bake at 300 degrees for 12 minutes. Top with peach halves. Fill peach cavities with cranberry sauce. Bake for 5 minutes longer. Yield: 6 servings.

Approx Per Serving:
Cal 371; Prot 9 g; Carbo 75 g; T Fat 5 g;
Chol 17 mg; Potas 495 mg; Sod 372 mg.

Ella Estepp, West Virginia

Microwave Dijon Ham

1/3 cup orange marmalade
1 1/2 tablespoons Dijon mustard
1/8 teaspoon cloves
1   1 1/2-pound cooked ham slice

Combine marmalade, mustard and cloves in bowl; mix well. Place ham slice in shallow glass baking dish. Brush with half the marmalade mixture. Microwave, loosely covered, on High for 4 minutes. Turn ham slice over; brush with remaining marmalade mixture. Microwave, uncovered, for 5 minutes. Let stand for 5 minutes. Yield: 4 servings.

Approx Per Serving:
Cal 487; Prot 37 g; Carbo 19 g; T Fat 29 g;
Chol 104 mg; Potas 656 mg; Sod 2097 mg.

Linda Tally, Texas

Microwave Upside-Down Ham Loaf

2 tablespoons butter	
1/2 cup drained crushed pineapple	
2 tablespoons brown sugar	
4 cups ground ham	
2 eggs, beaten	
2 tablespoons chopped onion	
1/2 cup bread crumbs	
1/2 cup pineapple juice	
1/2 teaspoon dry mustard	

Melt butter in 1 1/2-quart glass dish. Sprinkle pineapple and brown sugar into dish. Combine ham, eggs, onion, bread crumbs, pineapple juice and dry mustard in bowl; mix well. Pack lightly into prepared dish. Microwave on High for 15 minutes, turning dish 1/2 turn every 3 minutes. Invert onto serving plate.
Yield: 8 servings.

Approx Per Serving:
Cal 270; Prot 18 g; Carbo 12 g; T Fat 16 g;
Chol 120 mg; Potas 280 mg; Sod 920 mg.

Nancy S. Pope, Florida

Microwave Sausage Ring

1 egg	
2/3 cup milk	
3/4 cup oats	
1 1/2 pounds pork sausage, crumbled	
2/3 cup chopped peeled apple	
Basil, sage and salt to taste	
6 canned peach halves	

Mix egg, milk and oats in bowl. Let stand for 5 minutes. Add sausage, apple and seasonings; mix well. Arrange peach halves in glass ring mold or around custard cup inverted in 3-quart glass dish. Pack sausage mixture evenly into mold. Microwave, covered, on High for 17 minutes, turning dish once; drain. Let stand for 5 minutes. Invert onto serving platter. Serve with scrambled eggs in center if desired.
Yield: 6 servings.

Approx Per Serving:
Cal 358; Prot 10 g; Carbo 27 g; T Fat 24 g;
Chol 86 mg; Potas 279 mg; Sod 383 mg.

Sandra McRae, Arizona

Franks and Potatoes

4 frankfurters, thinly sliced	
1 1/2 cups drained sauerkraut	
4 medium potatoes, baked	
1 cup yogurt	

Brown frankfurter slices lightly in skillet over medium heat for 5 minutes. Add sauerkraut; mix well. Split potatoes. Spoon frankfurter mixture into potatoes. Top with yogurt.
Yield: 4 servings.

Approx Per Serving:
Cal 416; Prot 13 g; Carbo 59 g; T Fat 15 g;
Chol 30 mg; Potas 1157 mg; Sod 1131 mg.

Polly Reardon, Maryland

MACARONI AND FRANK SUPPER

1   16-ounce jar Cheez Whiz
1 pound frankfurters, sliced
3 cups macaroni, cooked
1   16-ounce can peas, drained
2 tablespoons finely chopped onion

Melt Cheez Whiz in saucepan over low heat. Add frankfurters, macaroni, peas and onion; mix well. Cook until heated through. Yield: 6 servings.

Approx Per Serving:
Cal 649; Prot 30 g; Carbo 39 g; T Fat 41 g; Chol 86 mg; Potas 535 mg; Sod 1910 mg.

Vivian W. Bennett, North Carolina

GERMAN PIZZA

1½ tablespoons margarine
3 medium potatoes, peeled, thinly sliced
Salt and pepper to taste
½ cup chopped onion
½ cup chopped green bell pepper
2 cups julienne ham strips
3 eggs, beaten
½ cup milk
½ cup shredded sharp Cheddar cheese

Melt margarine in 10-inch skillet. Layer potato slices, seasonings, onion, green pepper and ham ½ at a time in skillet. Cook, covered, over low heat for 20 minutes or until potatoes are tender. Beat eggs with milk. Pour evenly over layers. Cook, covered, until eggs are set. Top with cheese. Cook, covered, until cheese is melted. Cut into wedges to serve. Yield: 6 servings.

Approx Per Serving:
Cal 294; Prot 18 g; Carbo 16 g; T Fat 17 g; Chol 178 mg; Potas 462 mg; Sod 693 mg.

Norma Hetrick, Maryland

SKILLET QUICHE

1 pound sausage
12 eggs, beaten
1   10-ounce can Ro-Tel tomatoes
Salt and pepper to taste
1 cup shredded Cheddar cheese

Brown sausage in 10-inch skillet, stirring until crumbly; drain. Add eggs, tomatoes, salt and pepper. Cook until eggs are set, stirring frequently. Sprinkle with cheese. Cook, covered, until cheese is melted. Yield: 6 servings.

Approx Per Serving:
Cal 391; Prot 21 g; Carbo 4 g; T Fat 32 g; Chol 592 mg; Potas 325 mg; Sod 568 mg.

Janet Forrest Cousins, Arkansas

CLASSY QUICHE

Ingredients
1 unbaked 9-inch pie shell
8 ounces bacon, crisp-fried, crumbled
1 cup chopped Swiss cheese
1 4-ounce can chopped mushrooms, drained
1/4 cup chopped onion
1 10-ounce package frozen chopped broccoli, cooked
3 eggs
1 1/2 cups milk

Bake pie shell at 450 degrees for 5 minutes. Layer bacon, cheese, mushrooms, onion and broccoli in pie shell. Beat eggs and milk in bowl. Pour over layers. Bake at 325 degrees for 50 minutes or until center is set. Let stand for 10 minutes before serving. Yield: 6 servings.

Approx Per Serving:
Cal 533; Prot 26 g; Carbo 21 g; T Fat 39 g; Chol 194 mg; Potas 442 mg; Sod 987 mg.

Linda Hawbaker, Maryland

AMANDINE CHICKEN

Ingredients
2 cups chopped cooked chicken
1 cup chopped celery
1 tablespoon minced onion
1 cup cooked rice
1 can cream of chicken soup
3/4 cup mayonnaise
1 cup slivered almonds

Combine chicken, celery, onion, rice, soup and mayonnaise in bowl; mix well. Spoon into 2-quart baking dish. Top with almonds. Bake at 350 degrees for 40 minutes. May add 1 cup crushed cornflakes to topping if desired. Yield: 6 servings.

Approx Per Serving:
Cal 506; Prot 21 g; Carbo 18 g; T Fat 40 g; Chol 62 mg; Potas 392 mg; Sod 616 mg.

Madge Bullington, Kentucky

MICROWAVE APRICOT CHICKEN

Ingredients
5 pounds chicken pieces
1 envelope dry onion soup mix
1/4 cup mayonnaise
1/2 cup Russian salad dressing
1 8-ounce jar apricot preserves

Rinse chicken and pat dry. Arrange in glass baking dish. Microwave, covered, on High for 10 minutes. Turn chicken pieces over. Microwave on High for 10 minutes longer. Combine soup mix, mayonnaise, salad dressing and preserves in bowl; mix well. Spoon over chicken. Microwave for 2 minutes. Serve over rice. Yield: 8 servings.

Approx Per Serving:
Cal 501; Prot 43 g; Carbo 28 g; T Fat 24 g; Chol 141 mg; Potas 468 mg; Sod 1249 mg.

Nola Williams, South Dakota

BROCCOLI AND CHICKEN CASSEROLE

2 10-ounce packages frozen
broccoli, cooked, drained

1 cup rice, cooked

1 can cream of mushroom soup

2 7-ounce cans chunky
white chicken

8 ounces cream cheese, softened

1/4 cup milk

Combine broccoli, rice, soup, chicken and cream cheese in bowl; mix well. Spoon into baking dish. Pour milk over top. Bake at 350 degrees until bubbly. May top with shredded cheese if desired. Yield: 6 servings.

Approx Per Serving:
Cal 389; Prot 26 g; Carbo 19 g; T Fat 24 g;
Chol 105 mg; Potas 431 mg; Sod 611 mg.

Helen Jordan, North Dakota

CHICKEN WITH BROCCOLI AND STUFFING

4 cups chopped cooked chicken

2 cans cream of chicken soup

1 cup mayonnaise

1/4 teaspoon curry powder

1/2 cup melted butter

1 8-ounce package corn bread
stuffing mix

2 10-ounce packages frozen
broccoli, thawed

Place chicken in 9x13-inch baking dish. Combine soup, mayonnaise and curry powder in bowl; mix well. Combine butter and stuffing mix in bowl. Layer half the soup mixture and half the stuffing mixture over chicken. Arrange broccoli over layers. Top with remaining soup and stuffing. Bake at 350 degrees for 25 minutes. Yield: 8 servings.

Approx Per Serving:
Cal 584; Prot 27 g; Carbo 22 g; T Fat 44 g;
Chol 116 mg; Potas 409 mg; Sod 1207 mg.

Oma Lee Dixon, Kentucky

CHICKEN SPAGHETTI CASSEROLE

1 pound spaghetti, cooked

2 cups sour cream

2 8-ounce cans sliced
mushrooms, drained

Salt and pepper to taste

3 10-ounce packages frozen
chopped broccoli, cooked,
drained

1/4 cup slivered almonds

1 can cream of celery soup

4 cups chopped cooked chicken

1 cup shredded mozzarella cheese

Combine spaghetti, sour cream, mushrooms, salt and pepper in large baking dish. Mix broccoli, almonds and soup in bowl. Spread over spaghetti mixture. Top with chicken and cheese. Chill in refrigerator. Bake at 350 degrees until bubbly. Yield: 12 servings.

Approx Per Serving:
Cal 399; Prot 25 g; Carbo 38 g; T Fat 17 g;
Chol 69 mg; Potas 479 mg; Sod 467 mg.

Betty Davis, Tennessee

CHICKEN AND WILD RICE CASSEROLE

1   6-ounce package wild rice
3 cups chopped cooked chicken
1   16-ounce can French-style green beans, drained
1 cup mayonnaise
1 onion, chopped
1 can cream of celery soup

Cook rice using package directions. Combine with chicken, beans, mayonnaise, onion and soup in bowl; mix well. Spoon into baking dish. Bake at 350 degrees for 30 minutes or until bubbly. Yield: 8 servings.

Approx Per Serving:
Cal 419; Prot 18 g; Carbo 25 g; T Fat 28 g; Chol 67 mg; Potas 287 mg; Sod 633 mg.

Lucy Van Pelt, Alabama

RITZY CHICKEN CASSEROLE

1 cup butter cracker crumbs
4 cups chopped cooked chicken
2   10-ounce packages frozen Hawaiian-style mixed vegetables, thawed
8 ounces Velveeta cheese, chopped
1/2 cup butter
1 1/2 cups chicken broth
1 cup butter cracker crumbs

Sprinkle 1 cup cracker crumbs in greased 2-quart baking dish. Layer chicken and vegetables in prepared dish. Combine cheese, butter and chicken broth in saucepan. Cook over low heat until cheese and butter are melted, stirring frequently. Pour over layers. Top with remaining crumbs. Bake at 350 degrees for 1 hour or until bubbly. Yield: 8 servings.

Approx Per Serving:
Cal 494; Prot 31 g; Carbo 25 g; T Fat 33 g; Chol 121 mg; Potas 407 mg; Sod 942 mg.

Lynne Otwell, Alabama

SUPER CHICKEN CASSEROLE

4 cups chopped cooked chicken
1 can cream of chicken soup
8 ounces sour cream
1   8-ounce package corn bread stuffing mix
2 cups chicken broth

Place chicken in large baking dish. Mix soup and cream in bowl. Pour over chicken. Combine stuffing mix and chicken broth in bowl. Spread over casserole. Bake at 350 degrees for 45 minutes or until brown. Yield: 8 servings.

Approx Per Serving:
Cal 301; Prot 25 g; Carbo 16 g; T Fat 14 g; Chol 78 mg; Potas 335 mg; Sod 846 mg.

Jessie Davis, Tennessee

CHICKEN CREOLE

1 large onion, chopped

1 large green bell pepper, chopped

1 tablespoon oil

2 cups chopped cooked chicken

4 cups cooked rice

2 cups spaghetti sauce

Sauté onion and green pepper in oil in 3-quart saucepan. Stir in chicken, rice and spaghetti sauce. Simmer, covered, for 45 minutes. May bake at 350 degrees for 45 minutes if preferred. ·Yield: 6 servings.

Approx Per Serving:
Cal 361; Prot 18 g; Carbo 49 g; T Fat 10 g; Chol 42 mg; Potas 545 mg; Sod 453 mg.

Martha Dinwiddie, Kentucky

CROCK•POT CHICKEN

2 carrots, sliced

2 onions, sliced

2 stalks celery with leaves, sliced

3 pounds chicken pieces

1/2 cup chicken broth

1/2 cup water

Basil, salt and pepper to taste

Place carrots, onions and celery in Crock•Pot. Add chicken, chicken broth, water and seasonings. Cook on Low for 8 to 10 hours. Yield: 6 servings.

Approx Per Serving:
Cal 249; Prot 34 g; Carbo 7 g; T Fat 9 g; Chol 101 mg; Potas 491 mg; Sod 183 mg.

Jane H. Young, Tennessee

CURRIED BROILED CHICKEN

1/4 cup butter, softened

1 clove of garlic, crushed

Dry mustard, paprika, curry powder and salt to taste

4 chicken breasts

Cream butter with garlic and seasonings in bowl. Rinse chicken and pat dry. Spread with half the butter mixture. Place on rack in broiler pan. Broil on bottom rack of oven for 15 minutes or until brown. Turn chicken and spread with remaining butter. Broil for 15 minutes longer or until tender, basting frequently with pan drippings. Yield: 4 servings.

Approx Per Serving:
Cal 196; Prot 20 g; Carbo 0 g; T Fat 13 g; Chol 80 mg; Potas 224 mg; Sod 152 mg.

Sherrill Corley Weary, Illinois

CHICKEN DIVAN

2 10-ounce packages frozen broccoli, cooked
4 cups chopped cooked chicken
2 cans cream of chicken soup
1 cup mayonnaise
1/2 teaspoon curry powder
1 cup bread crumbs
2 tablespoons melted butter

Layer broccoli and chicken in greased 9x13-inch baking dish. Mix soup, mayonnaise and curry powder in bowl. Pour over chicken. Top with bread crumbs. Drizzle with butter. Bake, covered, at 350 degrees for 30 minutes. May top with cheese if desired. Yield: 10 servings.

Approx Per Serving:
Cal 396; Prot 21 g; Carbo 15 g; T Fat 28 g; Chol 75 mg; Potas 304 mg; Sod 759 mg.

Louise E. Beasley, Arkansas

ROASTED CHICKEN

2 broiler-fryers, cut up
4 cloves of garlic, crushed
1/2 cup olive oil
Salt and pepper to taste
Sweet Pepper Chutney (page 92)

Marinate chicken in mixture of garlic, olive oil, salt and pepper in bowl for 15 minutes. Drain, reserving marinade. Arrange chicken on rack in shallow baking dish. Bake at 450 degrees for 10 minutes, turning once. Reduce oven temperature to 350 degrees. Bake for 30 minutes or until tender, basting several times with reserved marinade. Serve chicken warm or chilled with Sweet Pepper Chutney. Yield: 6 to 8 servings.

Photograph for this recipe is on page 69.

HONOLULU CHICKEN

1 chicken, cut up
1 cup flour
Salt and pepper to taste
1/4 cup oil
1 10-ounce jar peach preserves
1/2 cup barbecue sauce
2 tablespoons soy sauce
1/2 cup chopped onion
1/2 cup chopped green bell pepper
1 7-ounce can sliced water chestnuts, drained

Rinse chicken and pat dry. Roll in mixture of flour, salt and pepper, coating well. Brown in oil in skillet; drain. Combine preserves, barbecue sauce, soy sauce and onion in bowl. Pour over chicken. Simmer for 30 minutes. Stir in green pepper and water chestnuts. Simmer for 10 minutes longer. Serve over rice. Yield: 5 servings.

Approx Per Serving:
Cal 646; Prot 44 g; Carbo 68 g; T Fat 22 g; Chol 121 mg; Potas 553 mg; Sod 742 mg.

Cindy Lipps, Tennessee

ITALIAN CHICKEN

4 chicken breasts

Salt and pepper to taste

2 tablespoons dry Italian salad
dressing mix

1 can cream of mushroom soup

6 ounces cream cheese, softened

1   4-ounce can mushrooms,
drained

1 tablespoon chopped onion

Sprinkle chicken with salt and pepper. Place in Crock•Pot. Sprinkle with salad dressing mix. Cook on Low for 5½ hours. Combine remaining ingredients in saucepan. Cook until onion is tender, stirring frequently. Pour over chicken. Cook for 30 minutes longer. Yield: 4 servings.

Approx Per Serving:
Cal 327; Prot 25 g; Carbo 8 g; T Fat 22 g;
Chol 96 mg; Potas 359 mg; Sod 918 mg.
Nutritional information does not include
salad dressing mix.

Maxine Hultman, Minnesota

LEMON CHICKEN

6 pounds chicken pieces

Pepper to taste

1   6-ounce can frozen
lemonade concentrate, thawed

½ cup margarine

6 cups crushed cornflakes

Sprinkle chicken with pepper. Combine with lemonade concentrate in bowl, turning to coat well. Let stand for 1 hour. Melt margarine in baking dish. Drain chicken. Roll in crumbs, coating well. Place in prepared dish. Bake at 350 degrees for 1 hour. Yield: 8 servings.

Approx Per Serving:
Cal 662; Prot 54 g; Carbo 54 g; T Fat 24 g;
Chol 152 mg; Potas 480 mg; Sod 912 mg.
Nutritional information includes entire
amount of lemonade concentrate.

Martha Parsons, Arizona

MEXICAN CHICKEN

4 cups chopped cooked chicken

Garlic powder and red pepper
to taste

1 onion, chopped

1   10-ounce can Ro-Tel tomatoes

1 can cream of mushroom soup

1 cup chicken broth

1 pound Velveeta cheese, chopped

2 cups crushed corn chips

Place chicken in 9x13-inch baking dish. Sprinkle with garlic powder, red pepper and onion. Combine Ro-Tel tomatoes, soup, broth and cheese in blender container. Process until smooth. Pour over chicken. Top with corn chips. Bake at 350 degrees for 45 minutes. Serve over rice. Yield: 8 servings.

Approx Per Serving:
Cal 441; Prot 35 g; Carbo 11 g; T Fat 28 g;
Chol 117 mg; Potas 436 mg; Sod 1392 mg.

Rheta Sampson, Kentucky

MICROWAVE ORANGE-GLAZED CHICKEN

3 pounds chicken pieces

1 6-ounce can frozen orange juice concentrate, thawed

1/2 cup drained chopped mushrooms

1 1/2 teaspoons cornstarch

1 teaspoon prepared mustard

1 1/2 teaspoons paprika

Rinse chicken and pat dry. Arrange in 7x12-inch glass baking dish. Combine remaining ingredients in bowl. Pour over chicken. Microwave, covered with waxed paper, on High for 18 minutes. Spoon pan juices over chicken. Microwave for 10 minutes longer or until chicken is tender. Yield: 4 servings.

Approx Per Serving:
Cal 400; Prot 51 g; Carbo 18 g; T Fat 13 g; Chol 152 mg; Potas 727 mg; Sod 246 mg.

Peg Hollenbeck, California

MICROWAVE CHICKEN ORIENTAL

6 chicken breasts, skinned

1/4 cup chopped onion

1/4 cup chopped green bell pepper

1/3 cup orange juice

1/3 cup catsup

2 tablespoons flour

2 tablespoons soy sauce

1 teaspoon prepared mustard

Garlic powder, salt and pepper to taste

Rinse chicken and pat dry. Arrange in 2-quart glass baking dish with thicker edges to outside. Top with onion and green pepper. Mix orange juice, catsup, flour, soy sauce, mustard and seasonings in bowl. Pour over chicken. Microwave, covered, on High for 20 to 24 minutes or until tender. Let stand for 5 minutes before serving. Garnish with orange slices. Yield: 6 servings.

Approx Per Serving:
Cal 131; Prot 21 g; Carbo 8 g; T Fat 1 g; Chol 49 mg; Potas 332 mg; Sod 566 mg.

Carolyn Jackson, Kansas

PEACHY CHICKEN

3 pounds chicken pieces

1/2 cup flour

Salt and pepper to taste

2 tablespoons melted margarine

1 8-count can refrigerator crescent rolls

1 29-ounce can sliced peaches, drained

Rinse chicken and pat dry. Coat with mixture of flour, salt and pepper. Place skin side down in margarine in 9x13-inch baking dish. Bake at 425 degrees for 45 minutes, turning chicken over after 30 minutes. Push chicken to 1 end of dish. Arrange prepared rolls in other end of dish. Top chicken with peaches. Bake for 13 minutes longer or until rolls are brown. Yield: 6 servings.

Approx Per Serving:
Cal 495; Prot 37 g; Carbo 43 g; T Fat 20 g; Chol 101 mg; Potas 504 mg; Sod 456 mg.

Deanna Cook, West Virginia

CHICKEN POTPIE

1/3 cup melted margarine

1/3 cup flour

Salt and pepper to taste

1 3/4 cups chicken broth

2/3 cup milk

2 cups chopped cooked chicken

1   10-ounce package frozen mixed vegetables, thawed

1 recipe 2-crust pie pastry

Blend margarine, flour, salt and pepper in saucepan. Cook over medium heat for 1 minute, stirring constantly. Stir in chicken broth and milk. Cook until thickened, stirring constantly. Stir in chicken and vegetables. Spoon into 2-quart pastry-lined baking dish. Top with remaining pastry. Seal edges; cut vents. Bake at 350 degrees for 30 minutes or until golden brown. Yield: 8 servings.

Approx Per Serving:
Cal 419; Prot 16 g; Carbo 30 g; T Fat 26 g; Chol 34 mg; Potas 249 mg; Sod 584 mg.

Susan Featherston, Kentucky

SPICY BAKED CHICKEN

3/4 cup flour

3/4 teaspoon paprika

1/2 teaspoon dried hot pepper flakes

2 tablespoons oil

4 chicken breast filets

Oregano, salt and pepper to taste

Mix flour with paprika and hot pepper flakes in bowl. Spread oil in baking dish. Rinse chicken and pat dry. Sprinkle with oregano, salt and pepper. Roll in oil in baking dish. Coat with flour mixture. Place in remaining oil in baking dish. Bake at 400 degrees for 20 minutes or until tender; do not turn. Yield: 4 servings.

Approx Per Serving:
Cal 239; Prot 22 g; Carbo 18 g; T Fat 8 g; Chol 49 mg; Potas 239 mg; Sod 55 mg.

Jacqui Bauer, Florida

CHICKEN SUPREME

8 chicken breast filets

8 slices bacon

1   8-ounce package dried beef, shredded

1 can cream of mushroom soup

1 cup sour cream

Rinse chicken and pat dry. Flatten with meat mallet. Roll as for jelly rolls. Wrap with bacon; secure with toothpicks. Sprinkle dried beef in Crock•Pot. Arrange chicken rolls over beef. Top with mixture of soup and sour cream. Cook on Low for 12 hours. Yield: 8 servings.

Approx Per Serving:
Cal 276; Prot 31 g; Carbo 5 g; T Fat 14 g; Chol 113 mg; Potas 440 mg; Sod 1462 mg.

Mary Eagon, Wisconsin

Recipes for this photograph are on pages 38, 65, 92 and 124.

ON-THE-GO LUNCHES

Relax and enjoy a tasty lunch break.

Broccoli and Cheddar Soup, 26

Tunaburgers, 44

Heavenly Banana Pudding, 121

Favorite Beverage

Shrimp and Spinach Salad, 34

Cheese Bread, 109

Oatmeal Cookie Bars, 139

Favorite Beverage

Microwave Coq au Vin

3 pounds chicken pieces

2 tablespoons melted margarine

1   16-ounce can small onions, drained

1   3-ounce can sliced mushrooms, drained

1   16-ounce can small potatoes, drained

2 tablespoons melted margarine

2 tablespoons flour

3/4 cup dry white wine

Thyme, garlic powder, salt and pepper to taste

Rinse chicken and pat dry. Coat with 2 tablespoons melted margarine in 7x11-inch glass baking dish. Microwave, covered, on High for 16 minutes, turning chicken once. Combine onions, mushrooms and potatoes with 2 tablespoons margarine in 8-inch glass dish. Microwave on High for 2 minutes. Stir in flour. Add wine and seasonings. Microwave for 4 minutes, stirring once. Pour over chicken. Microwave, covered, on High for 2 minutes. Garnish with parsley. Yield: 6 servings.

Approx Per Serving:
Cal 387; Prot 35 g; Carbo 19 g; T Fat 16 g; Chol 101 mg; Potas 614 mg; Sod 403 mg.

Shirlee Smith, California

Turkey Casserole

2   10-ounce packages frozen broccoli, thawed

10 slices cooked turkey

2 cans cream of chicken soup

3/4 cup mayonnaise

1 tablespoon lemon juice

1 cup shredded Cheddar cheese

Layer broccoli and turkey in 9x13-inch baking dish. Mix soup, mayonnaise and lemon juice in bowl. Pour over turkey. Top with cheese. Bake at 350 degrees for 40 minutes. Yield: 4 servings.

Approx Per Serving:
Cal 712; Prot 37 g; Carbo 21 g; T Fat 55 g; Chol 120 mg; Potas 619 mg; Sod 1691 mg.

Marianne Griffith, California

Turkey Chili

12 ounces ground turkey

1 clove of garlic, crushed

1 cup chopped onion

1 cup chopped green bell pepper

1/2 cup chopped celery

2 cups tomato juice

1 tablespoon chili powder

Cumin, oregano and salt to taste

Brown turkey with garlic, onion, green pepper and celery in saucepan, stirring constantly. Add tomato juice and seasonings; mix well. Cook, covered, over low heat for 35 minutes. Yield: 2 servings.

Approx Per Serving:
Cal 365; Prot 41 g; Carbo 20 g; T Fat 14 g; Chol 98 mg; Potas 1231 mg; Sod 1002 mg.

Marie Heltzel, Florida

EASY BAKED FISH

2 tablespoons Italian salad
dressing

1/4 cup lemon juice

1   8-ounce package potato
chips, crushed

1/4 cup Parmesan cheese

1 tablespoon parsley flakes

1 pound fish fillets

2 tablespoons oil

Mix salad dressing and lemon juice in shallow dish. Combine potato chip crumbs, Parmesan cheese and parsley flakes. Dip fish fillets in lemon juice mixture; roll in crumb mixture, coating well. Arrange on baking sheet. Drizzle with oil. Bake at 500 degrees for 10 to 15 minutes or until fish flakes easily.
Yield: 4 servings.

Approx Per Serving:
Cal 597; Prot 35 g; Carbo 32 g; T Fat 39 g;
Chol 75 mg; Potas 1309 mg; Sod 484 mg.

Rachel Palmer, Tennessee

FISH AND VEGETABLE DELIGHT

1   10-ounce package frozen
chopped broccoli, thawed

4 flounder fillets

1 small onion, sliced into rings

1 can cream of mushroom soup

1/4 cup Parmesan cheese

1 tablespoon lemon juice

1/8 teaspoon pepper

Layer broccoli, fish fillets and onion rings in 9x13-inch baking dish. Combine soup, Parmesan cheese, lemon juice and pepper in bowl; mix well. Pour over layers. Bake at 350 degrees for 15 minutes or until fish flakes easily.
Yield: 4 servings.

Approx Per Serving:
Cal 236; Prot 27 g; Carbo 12 g; T Fat 9 g;
Chol 59 mg; Potas 632 mg; Sod 811 mg.

Helen Walton, Kentucky

LINGUINE WITH CLAM SAUCE

2 small onions, finely chopped

3 cloves of garlic, minced

1/4 cup olive oil

1 green bell pepper, finely
chopped

3 tablespoons flour

1/2 cup milk

1   6-ounce can clams, drained

Oregano, salt and pepper
to taste

12 ounces linguine, cooked

Sauté onions and garlic in olive oil in saucepan. Stir in green pepper. Blend flour and milk in bowl. Stir into saucepan. Cook over low heat until thickened, stirring constantly. Add clams, oregano, salt and pepper. Spoon over linguine. Serve with Parmesan cheese. Yield: 4 servings.

Approx Per Serving:
Cal 544; Prot 24 g; Carbo 74 g; T Fat 17 g;
Chol 33 mg; Potas 646 mg; Sod 65 mg.

Rudy Filek, West Virginia

CRAB IMPERIAL

1   7-ounce can crab meat, flaked
1 cup mayonnaise
4 egg whites, stiffly beaten
Salt and pepper to taste
1/4 cup bread crumbs

Mix crab meat and mayonnaise in bowl. Fold in egg whites, salt and pepper. Spoon into baking dish. Sprinkle with bread crumbs. Bake at 350 degrees for 45 minutes. Yield: 6 servings.

Approx Per Serving:
Cal 322; Prot 10 g; Carbo 4 g; T Fat 30 g;
Chol 51 mg; Potas 173 mg; Sod 383 mg.

Annabel D. Osbourn, West Virginia

MICROWAVE SALMON DUMPLINGS

1   10-count can refrigerator biscuits
1   7-ounce can salmon, drained
1 can Cheddar cheese soup
1 cup milk
2 tablespoons flour
2 tablespoons chopped green bell pepper
1 tablespoon chopped parsley

Arrange biscuits in 1 1/2-quart glass baking dish. Combine salmon, soup, milk, flour, green pepper and parsley in bowl; mix well. Spoon over biscuits. Microwave on High for 12 minutes, basting once. Yield: 4 servings.

Approx Per Serving:
Cal 225; Prot 15 g; Carbo 15 g; T Fat 12 g;
Chol 56 mg; Potas 412 mg; Sod 677 mg.

Ruth Lund, Wisconsin

SALMON FLORENTINE

1 medium onion, chopped
2 tablespoons butter
Salt and pepper to taste
2 tablespoons flour
1 cup milk
2   10-ounce packages frozen chopped spinach, cooked, drained
1   7-ounce can salmon, drained
2 tablespoons flour
1 cup milk
1 cup shredded Cheddar cheese

Sauté onion in butter in skillet. Stir in seasonings and 2 tablespoons flour. Add 1 cup milk gradually. Cook until thickened, stirring constantly. Stir in spinach. Spoon into pie plate. Flake salmon over spinach mixture. Blend remaining 2 tablespoons flour and 1 cup milk in saucepan. Stir in cheese. Cook until thickened, stirring constantly. Pour over salmon. Bake at 350 degrees for 15 minutes or until bubbly. Yield: 6 servings.

Approx Per Serving:
Cal 265; Prot 18 g; Carbo 15 g; T Fat 16 g;
Chol 56 mg; Potas 581 mg; Sod 443 mg.

Margaret Greer, Florida

SHRIMP AND BROCCOLI CASSEROLE

1 pound fresh broccoli, chopped
1 pound frozen peeled shrimp
1 can cream of mushroom soup
1/2 cup mayonnaise
1/2 teaspoon lemon juice
3/4 teaspoon curry powder
1/2 cup shredded Cheddar cheese

Cook broccoli in a small amount of water in saucepan for 10 minutes; drain. Cook shrimp in boiling water to cover in saucepan for 5 minutes; drain. Layer broccoli and shrimp in baking dish. Mix next 4 ingredients in bowl. Spoon over layers. Bake at 325 degrees for 20 minutes. Top with cheese. Bake for 10 minutes longer. Yield: 4 servings.

Approx Per Serving:
Cal 475; Prot 32 g; Carbo 13 g; T Fat 34 g; Chol 253 mg; Potas 650 mg; Sod 1146 mg.

Donna Wright, Minnesota

EASY MICROWAVE SHRIMP CREOLE

1   16-ounce can tomatoes, chopped
1 green bell pepper, chopped
1 medium onion, chopped
1 bay leaf
Chili powder, salt and pepper to taste
1 pound fresh shrimp, peeled

Combine tomatoes, green pepper, onion, bay leaf and seasonings in 1 1/2-quart glass dish. Microwave, covered, on High for 8 to 12 minutes or until bubbly, stirring once. Stir in shrimp. Microwave, covered, on High for 3 to 5 minutes or just until shrimp are pink; do not overcook. Let stand for 3 to 5 minutes; remove bay leaf. Serve over rice. Yield: 4 servings.

Approx Per Serving:
Cal 154; Prot 25 g; Carbo 9 g; T Fat 2 g; Chol 221 mg; Potas 567 mg; Sod 440 mg.

Martha Goad, Tennessee

SHRIMP STIR-FRY

1 tablespoon margarine
1   10-ounce package frozen snow peas
8 ounces fresh mushrooms, sliced
1 green bell pepper, chopped
2 tablespoons margarine
8 ounces shrimp, peeled, cooked
1   10-ounce can pineapple chunks, drained

Heat 1 tablespoon margarine to 220 degrees in wok. Add snow peas. Stir-fry until tender. Remove with slotted spoon. Repeat process with mushrooms and green pepper, using remaining margarine. Return all vegetables to wok. Add shrimp and pineapple. Stir-fry until heated through. Yield: 2 servings.

Approx Per Serving:
Cal 452; Prot 32 g; Carbo 40 g; T Fat 20 g; Chol 225 mg; Potas 1190 mg; Sod 442 mg.

Jenny Dobbs, Pennsylvania

Broccoli and Tuna Casserole

1   10-ounce package frozen
      chopped broccoli

1   6-ounce can water-pack
      tuna, drained

1 can cream of mushroom soup

1/2 soup can milk

1/2 cup crushed potato chips

1/2 cup shredded Cheddar
      cheese

Cook broccoli using package directions; drain. Layer broccoli and tuna in 1 1/2-quart baking dish. Pour mixture of soup and milk over layers. Sprinkle with potato chips and cheese. Bake at 350 degrees for 15 minutes. Yield: 4 servings.

Approx Per Serving:
Cal 252; Prot 21 g; Carbo 13 g; T Fat 13 g;
Chol 45 mg; Potas 423 mg; Sod 905 mg.

Lois Edwards, Kentucky

Microwave Savory Tuna Casserole

1 cup elbow macaroni, cooked

3/4 cup frozen green peas,
      cooked

1 can cream of celery soup

1   3-ounce can French-fried
      onions

1/3 cup creamy Italian
      salad dressing

1   7-ounce can tuna, drained

3/4 cup shredded Cheddar
      cheese

Combine macaroni, peas, soup, onion, salad dressing and tuna in bowl; mix well. Spoon into 3-quart baking dish. Microwave on Medium-High for 7 to 10 minutes or until bubbly. Top with cheese. Let stand for 3 minutes or until cheese is melted. Yield: 5 servings.

Approx Per Serving:
Cal 380; Prot 20 g; Carbo 24 g; T Fat 24 g;
Chol 38 mg; Potas 226 mg; Sod 832 mg.

Kathy Bengstrom, Minnesota

Tuna Quiche

1 unbaked deep-dish pie shell

1   7-ounce can tuna, drained

1 1/2 cups shredded Swiss cheese

1/2 cup finely chopped onion

2 eggs, beaten

1 cup evaporated milk

1 tablespoon lemon juice

1 teaspoon chopped chives

Garlic salt, salt and pepper
      to taste

Prick bottom and sides of pie shell with fork. Bake at 450 degrees for 5 minutes. Layer tuna, cheese and onion in pie shell. Beat eggs, evaporated milk, lemon juice, chives and seasonings in bowl. Pour over layers. Bake at 450 degrees for 15 minutes. Reduce temperature to 350 degrees. Bake for 12 minutes longer or until golden brown. Yield: 6 servings.

Approx Per Serving:
Cal 411; Prot 25 g; Carbo 20 g; T Fat 26 g;
Chol 135 mg; Potas 287 mg; Sod 442 mg.

Clara Richardson, Tennessee

Tuna Pizza Quiches

3 7-ounce cans tuna, drained

½ teaspoon oregano

½ cup chopped green
bell pepper

2 cups shredded mozzarella
cheese

½ cup Parmesan cheese

2 10-ounce cans pizza sauce

2 baked 8-inch pie shells

Combine tuna, oregano and green pepper in bowl; mix well. Combine cheeses in small bowl. Alternate layers of tuna mixture, pizza sauce and cheeses in pie shells until all ingredients are used, ending with cheeses. Bake at 350 degrees for 25 to 30 minutes or until set. Yield: 12 servings.

Approx Per Serving:
Cal 370; Prot 22 g; Carbo 22 g; T Fat 21 g; Chol 26 mg; Potas 324 mg; Sod 727 mg.

Mona Ringer, Florida

Chilies Rellenos

1 20-ounce can chili peppers,
split, seeded

1 pound Cheddar cheese,
shredded

1 pound Monterey Jack cheese,
shredded

6 eggs, beaten

1 6-ounce can evaporated milk

Place half the chili peppers in 9x13-inch baking dish. Top with cheeses and remaining peppers. Beat eggs with evaporated milk in bowl. Pour over layers. Bake at 350 degrees for 1 hour or until set and light brown. Serve with salsa. Yield: 8 servings.

Approx Per Serving:
Cal 556; Prot 35 g; Carbo 10 g; T Fat 42 g; Chol 323 mg; Potas 456 mg; Sod 734 mg.

Todd Coburn, California

Mexican Haystacks

3 16-ounce cans kidney beans

1 16-ounce can chili beans

1 16-ounce package corn chips

1 head lettuce, shredded

2 tomatoes, chopped

2 cups shredded Cheddar
cheese

Combine beans in saucepan. Cook until heated through. Spread corn chips on serving plates. Layer beans, lettuce, tomatoes and cheese over chips. Serve immediately. May add toppings such as olives, guacamole, sour cream or salsa if desired. Yield: 8 servings.

Approx Per Serving:
Cal 616; Prot 23 g; Carbo 68 g; T Fat 28 g; Chol 30 mg; Potas 811 mg; Sod 1432 mg.
Nutritional information does not
include unlisted toppings.

Becky Lane, Minnesota

QUICK LASAGNA

4 ounces wide noodles, cooked

1 cup cream-style cottage cheese

1   15-ounce can spaghetti sauce

1/4 cup shredded Cheddar
cheese

Layer noodles, cottage cheese, spaghetti sauce and Cheddar cheese in greased shallow baking dish. Bake at 375 degrees for 25 minutes. Yield: 4 servings.

Approx Per Serving:
Cal 305; Prot 14 g; Carbo 40 g; T Fat 10 g; Chol 15 mg; Potas 460 mg; Sod 786 mg.

Ron Seath, Minnesota

LASAGNA ROLL-UPS

1   10-ounce package frozen
chopped broccoli, thawed

16 ounces ricotta cheese

1/4 cup Parmesan cheese

1/2 teaspoon salt

1 egg

8 ounces lasagna noodles,
cooked

1   21-ounce jar Italian sauce

1 cup shredded mozzarella
cheese

Combine broccoli, ricotta cheese, Parmesan cheese, salt and egg in bowl; mix well. Place noodles in single layer on waxed paper. Spread broccoli mixture on each noodle. Roll as for jelly rolls. Pour 3/4 of the Italian sauce into 8x12-inch baking dish. Place rolled noodles in sauce. Top with and remaining sauce and mozzarella cheese. Bake, loosely covered with foil, at 375 degrees for 30 minutes or until bubbly. Yield: 6 servings.

Approx Per Serving:
Cal 477; Prot 23 g; Carbo 49 g; T Fat 21 g; Chol 101 mg; Potas 572 mg; Sod 892 mg.

Linda Junkin, Georgia

LINGUINE AND BROCCOLI WITH CREAM

2 1/2 cups broccoli flowerets

1 cup finely chopped parsley

3 cloves of garlic, minced

3 tablespoons oil

2 cups half and half

12 ounces linguine, cooked

1 cup Parmesan cheese

Stir-fry broccoli, parsley and garlic in oil in skillet for 2 minutes or until broccoli is tender-crisp. Add half and half. Heat just to serving temperature; do not boil. Place linguine in serving bowl. Pour broccoli mixture over top. Sprinkle with cheese; toss lightly. Yield: 4 servings.

Approx Per Serving:
Cal 676; Prot 25 g; Carbo 74 g; T Fat 32 g; Chol 60 mg; Potas 641 mg; Sod 448 mg.

Sarah Beard, Pennsylvania

BROCCOLI AND MACARONI DINNER

2 cloves of garlic, minced
2 tablespoons olive oil
2 10-ounce packages frozen chopped broccoli, cooked
1 7-ounce package macaroni and cheese dinner, prepared
Salt and pepper to taste

Sauté garlic in olive oil in saucepan for 2 minutes. Stir in broccoli, macaroni and cheese and seasonings. Spoon into baking dish. Bake at 350 degrees for 15 to 20 minutes or until bubbly. Yield: 6 servings.

Approx Per Serving:
Cal 261; Prot 9 g; Carbo 28 g; T Fat 13 g; Chol 0 mg; Potas 174 mg; Sod 349 mg.

Dorothye Jones, Florida

VEGETARIAN CHILI

2/3 cup chopped onion
1 green bell pepper, chopped
1 tablespoon oil
1 cup bouillon
1 28-ounce can tomatoes
1 10-ounce can corn
1 16-ounce can kidney beans
1 8-ounce can tomato sauce
1 tablespoon chili powder
Garlic powder, cumin and pepper to taste

Sauté onion and green pepper in oil in 4-quart saucepan. Add bouillon, tomatoes, corn, beans, tomato sauce and seasonings; mix well. Bring to a boil; reduce heat. Simmer, covered, for 1 hour or to desired consistency. May serve over hot pasta if desired. Yield: 6 servings.

Approx Per Serving:
Cal 169; Prot 8 g; Carbo 31 g; T Fat 4 g; Chol 0 mg; Potas 780 mg; Sod 947 mg.

Mrs. John Jarvis, Kentucky

CHEESE AND EGGS SPAGHETTI

8 ounces spaghetti, cooked
6 hard-boiled eggs, cut into halves
1 can tomato soup
8 ounces American cheese, chopped
1 small onion, minced
Salt and parsley flakes to taste

Place spaghetti in serving dish. Arrange eggs on spaghetti. Combine soup, cheese, onion, salt and parsley flakes in saucepan. Cook over low heat until cheese is melted, stirring constantly. Pour over spaghetti. Serve immediately. Yield: 4 servings.

Approx Per Serving:
Cal 601; Prot 30 g; Carbo 57 g; T Fat 28 g; Chol 465 mg; Potas 521 mg; Sod 1445 mg.

Nelda Pointer, Louisiana

Versatile Vegetables
& Side Dishes

Microwave Baked Beans

1	31-ounce can pork and beans
	1/4 cup catsup
	1/4 cup packed brown sugar
	2 tablespoons mustard
	2 tablespoons molasses
	Onion flakes, salt and pepper to taste
	4 slices bacon

Combine beans, catsup, brown sugar, mustard, molasses and seasonings in 8x8-inch glass dish. Microwave on High for 10 minutes, rotating dish and stirring after 5 minutes. Place bacon on microwave bacon pan. Microwave on High for 4 minutes. Microwave for 3 minutes longer. Arrange bacon over beans. Yield: 8 servings.

Approx Per Serving:
Cal 189; Prot 7 g; Carbo 35 g; T Fat 3 g; Chol 10 mg; Potas 514 mg; Sod 565 mg.

Gail Moore, Mississippi

Santa Fe Bean Pot

	1/4 cup chopped onion
	1 clove of garlic, minced
	1 tablespoon butter
1	16-ounce can barbecued beans
	1/2 cup canned corn
	1/2 teaspoon horseradish

Sauté onion and garlic in butter in saucepan. Stir in beans, corn and horseradish. Heat to serving temperature, stirring occasionally. Yield: 2 servings.

Approx Per Serving:
Cal 346; Prot 14 g; Carbo 57 g; T Fat 10 g; Chol 31 mg; Potas 709 mg; Sod 906 mg.

Gladys Morgan, Illinois

Easy Green Bean Casserole

1	16-ounce can green beans, drained
	1 onion, chopped
	1 can Cheddar cheese soup
	1 soup can milk
	Salt and pepper to taste

Combine beans and onion in bowl. Stir in soup, milk and seasonings. Spoon into 2-quart baking dish. Bake at 350 degrees for 30 minutes. Yield: 4 servings.

Approx Per Serving:
Cal 174; Prot 8 g; Carbo 18 g; T Fat 9 g; Chol 28 mg; Potas 379 mg; Sod 887 mg.

Edna Upton, Oklahoma

Macaroni and Green Beans

1 7-ounce package macaroni and cheese dinner mix

1/2 cup milk

1 can cream of mushroom soup

2 10-ounce packages frozen green beans, thawed

1 3-ounce can French-fried onions

Prepare macaroni and cheese dinner according to package directions, using 1/2 cup milk. Combine with soup and green beans in baking dish; mix well. Top with onions. Bake at 350 degrees for 30 minutes. Yield: 6 servings.

Approx Per Serving:
Cal 258; Prot 9 g; Carbo 39 g; T Fat 9 g; Chol 8 mg; Potas 167 mg; Sod 725 mg.

Laverne Mynes, Maryland

Oriental Green Beans

2 10-ounce packages frozen green beans

1/2 cup water

1/2 teaspoon salt

1 7-ounce can sliced water chestnuts, drained

Combine green beans with water and salt in saucepan. Cook for 8 minutes or until tender-crisp. Add water chestnuts. Cook until heated through. Yield: 8 servings.

Approx Per Serving:
Cal 31; Prot 1 g; Carbo 7 g; T Fat 0 g; Chol 0 mg; Potas 108 mg; Sod 144 mg.

Soowan Han Scheuermann, California

Original Green Bean Casserole

2 16-ounce cans green beans, drained

1 can cream of mushroom soup

3/4 cup milk

1/2 teaspoon pepper

1 3-ounce can French-fried onions

Combine beans, soup, milk, pepper and half the onions in bowl; mix well. Spoon into 1 1/2-quart baking dish. Bake at 350 degrees for 30 minutes. Top with remaining onions. Bake for 5 minutes longer. Yield: 6 servings.

Approx Per Serving:
Cal 147; Prot 4 g; Carbo 17 g; T Fat 8 g; Chol 10 mg; Potas 239 mg; Sod 827 mg.

Marsha Sims, Texas

KIDNEY BEAN CASSEROLE

1/2 cup chopped green bell pepper

1/2 cup chopped onion

1 tablespoon margarine

2 16-ounce cans kidney beans, drained

1/4 cup catsup

6 ounces cream cheese, softened

Salt and pepper to taste

Sauté green pepper and onion in margarine in skillet. Stir in beans, catsup and cream cheese. Bring to a boil, stirring constantly. Stir in salt and pepper. Simmer, covered, until of desired consistency. Yield: 6 servings.

Approx Per Serving:
Cal 257; Prot 10 g; Carbo 28 g; T Fat 12 g; Chol 31 mg; Potas 502 mg; Sod 750 mg.

Lydia Musgrove, Missouri

SWEET AND SOUR GREEN BEANS

3 slices bacon

2 15-ounce cans green beans, drained

1 tablespoon minced onion

1/2 teaspoon sugar

1 tablespoon vinegar

Dillweed and pepper to taste

1/2 cup water

Fry bacon in skillet until crisp. Remove bacon and crumble. Stir green beans into drippings. Add onion, sugar, vinegar, seasonings and water. Simmer until heated through. Spoon into serving dish. Sprinkle with bacon.
Yield: 6 servings.

Approx Per Serving:
Cal 48; Prot 3 g; Carbo 7 g; T Fat 2 g; Chol 3 mg; Potas 175 mg; Sod 407 mg.

Ann Fitz-Simons, North Carolina

ORANGE BEETS

1 6-ounce can frozen orange juice concentrate

1 juice can beet liquid

3/4 cup cider vinegar

11/4 cups packed brown sugar

2 tablespoons cornstarch

1 tablespoon margarine

1 29-ounce can beets, drained

Combine orange juice concentrate, beet liquid, vinegar, brown sugar, cornstarch and margarine in saucepan. Cook over medium heat until thickened and smooth, stirring constantly. Add beets. Cook until heated through.
Yield: 6 servings.

Approx Per Serving:
Cal 286; Prot 2 g; Carbo 68 g; T Fat 2 g; Chol 0 mg; Potas 575 mg; Sod 404 mg.

Patricia Kovak, Kansas

CREAMY BROCCOLI CASSEROLE

3 10-ounce packages frozen
   chopped broccoli

2 cups shredded Cheddar
   cheese

1 cup mayonnaise

1 can cream of mushroom soup

2 small onions, chopped

2 eggs, beaten

Steam broccoli in saucepan until tender; drain. Combine with cheese, mayonnaise, soup, onions and eggs in bowl; mix well. Spoon into buttered baking dish. Bake at 350 degrees for 45 minutes. Yield: 8 servings.

Approx Per Serving:
Cal 409; Prot 13 g; Carbo 12 g; T Fat 36 g;
Chol 115 mg; Potas 317 mg; Sod 683 mg.

Nancy Voogd, California

MICROWAVE BROCCOLI AND CHEESE CASSEROLE

1 10-ounce package frozen
   chopped broccoli

1 small onion, chopped

1 can cream of chicken soup

1/2 cup Cheez Whiz

1/2 cup minute rice

Salt and pepper to taste

Place broccoli in 1-quart glass dish. Microwave, covered, on High for 3 minutes, turning dish once; drain. Add onion; mix lightly. Microwave for 3 minutes longer. Stir in soup. Microwave, covered, for 3 minutes. Stir in Cheez Whiz, rice and seasonings. Microwave for 2 minutes or until bubbly. Let stand, covered, until rice is tender. Yield: 4 servings.

Approx Per Serving:
Cal 191; Prot 8 g; Carbo 22 g; T Fat 8 g;
Chol 15 mg; Potas 287 mg; Sod 785 mg.

Annette Sams, Colorado

BROCCOLI AND RICE CASSEROLE

1 small onion, chopped

2 stalks celery, chopped

1 tablespoon butter

1 10-ounce package frozen
   broccoli, thawed

2 cups cooked rice

1 can cream of chicken soup

1 cup shredded Cheddar cheese

Sauté onion and celery in butter in skillet. Stir in broccoli, rice and soup. Spoon into greased 9x13-inch baking dish. Sprinkle with cheese. Bake at 450 degrees for 15 minutes.
Yield: 6 servings.

Approx Per Serving:
Cal 236; Prot 9 g; Carbo 25 g; T Fat 11 g;
Chol 29 mg; Potas 227 mg; Sod 556 mg.

Mildred Skala, California

CARROT AND APPLE CASSEROLE

6 tablespoons sugar
2 tablespoons flour
1/4 teaspoon salt
5 apples, thinly sliced
2 cups sliced peeled carrots
3/4 cup orange juice

Combine sugar, flour and salt in bowl. Alternate layers of apples and carrots in baking dish, sprinkling each layer with sugar mixture. Pour orange juice over layers. Bake at 350 degrees for 20 to 30 minutes or until carrots are tender-crisp. Yield: 4 servings.

Approx Per Serving:
Cal 231; Prot 2 g; Carbo 59 g; T Fat 1 g;
Chol 0 mg; Potas 470 mg; Sod 154 mg.

Candy Overton, Texas

CANDIED CARROTS

2 tablespoons butter
1 16-ounce can small whole carrots, drained
2 tablespoons brown sugar
Nutmeg to taste

Melt butter in saucepan. Add carrots. Sprinkle with brown sugar and nutmeg. Simmer, covered, for 10 minutes. Cook, uncovered, for 5 minutes longer or until carrots are glazed, stirring frequently. Yield: 4 servings.

Approx Per Serving:
Cal 125; Prot 1 g; Carbo 18 g; T Fat 6 g;
Chol 16 mg; Potas 392 mg; Sod 91 mg.

Barbara Conmy, Florida

KID'S CARROTS

1 1/2 pounds carrots, sliced
1/2 cup raisins
1/4 cup butter
Cinnamon, nutmeg and salt to taste
2 tablespoons brown sugar

Combine carrots, raisins, butter, cinnamon, nutmeg and salt in saucepan. Cook over medium heat for 10 minutes or until carrots are tender, stirring occasionally. Stir in brown sugar until dissolved. Yield: 6 servings.

Approx Per Serving:
Cal 175; Prot 2 g; Carbo 27 g; T Fat 8 g;
Chol 21 mg; Potas 488 mg; Sod 107 mg.

Evelyn Bradon, Louisiana

Marinated Carrots

2 pounds carrots, sliced, cooked

½ cup chopped celery

½ cup chopped green bell pepper

1 cup sugar

1 can tomato soup

2 teaspoons Worcestershire sauce

½ cup oil

1 teaspoon prepared mustard

Combine vegetables in bowl. Mix sugar, soup, Worcestershire sauce, oil and mustard in saucepan. Bring to a boil. Pour over vegetables. Chill overnight. May serve hot if preferred. Yield: 10 servings.

Approx Per Serving:
Cal 400; Prot 5 g; Carbo 66 g; T Fat 15 g; Chol 0 mg; Potas 896 mg; Sod 1929 mg.

Ronda Tackett, Texas

Sweet Carrots

1 pound carrots, sliced ½ inch thick

¼ cup sugar

¼ cup butter

Combine carrots and sugar with water to cover in 2-quart saucepan. Cook until tender; drain. Add butter; mix gently until butter is melted and carrots are coated. Yield: 4 servings.

Approx Per Serving:
Cal 199; Prot 1 g; Carbo 24 g; T Fat 12 g; Chol 31 mg; Potas 371 mg; Sod 136 mg.

Cindy Glaston, Georgia

Fried Carrots and Corn

8 ounces carrots, sliced ½ inch thick

1 small onion, chopped

1 small green bell pepper, chopped

3 tablespoons melted butter

1   17-ounce can corn, drained

Sauté carrots, onion and green pepper in butter in skillet over medium heat until tender. Stir in corn. Cook until heated through. Yield: 4 servings.

Approx Per Serving:
Cal 212; Prot 4 g; Carbo 31 g; T Fat 10 g; Chol 23 mg; Potas 455 mg; Sod 373 mg.

Jenny Miller, West Virginia

MICROWAVE CAULIFLOWER

1 head cauliflower
2 tablespoons water
1/2 cup mayonnaise
1 teaspoon Dijon mustard
1 teaspoon minced onion
1/2 cup shredded Cheddar cheese

Place trimmed cauliflower in glass casserole. Add water. Microwave, covered, on High for 8 minutes. Spread with mixture of mayonnaise, mustard and onion. Microwave on Medium-High for 1 1/2 minutes. Sprinkle with cheese. Let stand for 5 minutes. Yield: 4 servings.

Approx Per Serving:
Cal 450; Prot 16 g; Carbo 7 g; T Fat 41 g; Chol 76 mg; Potas 424 mg; Sod 537 mg.

Wilma Jefferson, Kansas

CREAMY CORN

3 ounces cream cheese, softened
1/4 cup milk
1 tablespoon margarine, softened
1/2 teaspoon onion salt
1 16-ounce can whole kernel corn, drained

Combine cream cheese, milk, margarine and onion salt in small saucepan. Cook over low heat until cream cheese and margarine are melted. Stir in corn. Cook until heated through, stirring constantly. Yield: 6 servings.

Approx Per Serving:
Cal 133; Prot 3 g; Carbo 15 g; T Fat 8 g; Chol 17 mg; Potas 148 mg; Sod 421 mg.

Eunice Lawrence, Alabama

FOUR-CORN SPECIAL

1/2 cup margarine
8 ounces cream cheese, softened
1 16-ounce can whole kernel corn
1 16-ounce can Shoe Peg corn, drained
1 12-ounce can Mexicorn, drained
1 16-ounce can cream-style corn

Melt margarine and cream cheese in 2-quart saucepan; mix well. Drain whole kernel corn, reserving liquid. Add all corn to cream cheese mixture. Add enough reserved liquid to make of desired consistency. Simmer over low heat until heated through. Yield: 8 servings.

Approx Per Serving:
Cal 367; Prot 7 g; Carbo 40 g; T Fat 23 g; Chol 31 mg; Potas 356 mg; Sod 741 mg.

Margaret Olson, Minnesota

Mexican Corn

8 ounces cream cheese

2 tablespoons butter

1/4 cup milk

1/4 teaspoon garlic salt

2 16-ounce cans whole kernel corn, drained

2 4-ounce cans chopped green chilies

Combine cream cheese, butter, milk and garlic salt in saucepan. Cook over low heat until cream cheese and butter are melted; mix well. Stir in corn and chilies. Spoon into greased baking dish. Bake at 350 degrees for 20 minutes or until bubbly. Yield: 6 servings.

Approx Per Serving:
Cal 303; Prot 7 g; Carbo 32 g; T Fat 19 g; Chol 53 mg; Potas 372 mg; Sod 593 mg.

Mary Wynne Eisenberg, Maryland

Microwave Corn Casserole

2 16-ounce cans white corn, drained

8 ounces sour cream

1 4-ounce can sliced mushrooms, drained

Salt and pepper to taste

1/2 cup shredded Cheddar cheese

Combine corn, sour cream, mushrooms, salt and pepper in glass dish; mix well. Microwave on High until bubbly. Sprinkle with cheese. Let stand for 5 minutes. Yield: 6 servings.

Approx Per Serving:
Cal 245; Prot 8 g; Carbo 31 g; T Fat 13 g; Chol 27 mg; Potas 320 mg; Sod 509 mg.

Mikka Spears, Texas

Glorified Peas

2 10-ounce packages frozen peas, cooked

1 4-ounce jar chopped pimentos, drained

1 cup milk

1/2 teaspoon salt

2 tablespoons chopped onion

8 ounces cream cheese, softened

Mix peas and pimentos lightly in buttered 8x11-inch baking dish. Combine milk, salt, onion and cream cheese in blender container. Process until smooth. Pour over vegetables. Bake at 350 degrees for 30 minutes. Yield: 8 servings.

Approx Per Serving:
Cal 178; Prot 7 g; Carbo 13 g; T Fat 11 g; Chol 35 mg; Potas 197 mg; Sod 292 mg.

Wanda Stafford, Virginia

EASY SCALLOPED POTATOES

1 large onion, sliced
6 slices bacon, chopped
6 potatoes, cooked, sliced
Salt and pepper to taste
1 can Cheddar cheese soup
1 cup shredded Cheddar cheese

Sauté onion with bacon in skillet, stirring until bacon is crisp; drain. Combine with potatoes in greased baking dish. Season with salt and pepper. Pour soup over top; mix gently. Sprinkle with cheese. Bake at 350 degrees until bubbly. Yield: 8 servings.

Approx Per Serving:
Cal 302; Prot 10 g; Carbo 43 g; T Fat 10 g; Chol 28 mg; Potas 747 mg; Sod 460 mg.

Melinda Vantrease, South Carolina

SPICY POTATOES

1 2-pound package frozen French-fried potatoes
1/3 cup melted butter
3 tablespoons (or more) taco seasoning mix
Salt and pepper to taste

Toss potatoes with butter in bowl, coating well. Arrange in single layer on baking sheet. Sprinkle with seasonings. Bake at 400 degrees for 15 to 20 minutes or until crisp and brown. Yield: 10 servings.

Approx Per Serving:
Cal 126; Prot 2 g; Carbo 16 g; T Fat 6 g; Chol 16 mg; Potas 279 mg; Sod 348 mg.

Deonne Farmer, Texas

POTATO SQUARES

1/4 cup margarine
2 cups shredded Cheddar cheese
10 medium potatoes, boiled, peeled, grated
1 cup sour cream
1/3 cup chopped onion
Salt and pepper to taste

Melt margarine in saucepan. Stir in cheese. Heat until cheese melts. Combine with potatoes in bowl. Add sour cream, onion and seasonings; mix well. Spoon into greased shallow 3-quart baking dish. Bake at 350 degrees for 30 minutes. Garnish with paprika if desired. Cut into squares to serve. Yield: 12 servings.

Approx Per Serving:
Cal 249; Prot 7 g; Carbo 24 g; T Fat 14 g; Chol 28 mg; Potas 424 mg; Sod 178 mg.

Melissa Angell, Texas

SPINACH DELIGHT

1 can cream of potato soup

1 cup sour cream

2 10-ounce packages frozen chopped spinach, thawed, drained

1 cup shredded Monterey Jack cheese

Combine soup and sour cream in bowl. Stir in spinach. Spoon into 8x8-inch baking dish. Bake at 350 degrees for 25 minutes. Sprinkle with cheese. Bake for 5 minutes longer.
Yield: 6 servings.

Approx Per Serving:
Cal 208; Prot 9 g; Carbo 11 g; T Fat 15 g; Chol 37 mg; Potas 407 mg; Sod 607 mg.

Deena Harmon, Arkansas

IMPOSSIBLE VEGETABLE PIE

2 cups chopped fresh broccoli

1/2 cup chopped onion

1/2 cup chopped green bell pepper

1 cup shredded Cheddar cheese

1 1/2 cups milk

3/4 cup baking mix

3 eggs

Salt and pepper to taste

Cook broccoli in a small amount of water in saucepan for 5 minutes; drain. Combine with onion, green pepper and cheese in bowl. Spoon into greased pie plate. Combine milk, baking mix, eggs and seasonings in blender container; process until smooth. Pour over vegetables. Bake at 400 degrees for 35 to 40 minutes on until knife inserted near center comes out clean. Let stand for 5 minutes before serving.
Yield: 6 servings.

Approx Per Serving:
Cal 235; Prot 12 g; Carbo 17 g; T Fat 14 g; Chol 165 mg; Potas 288 mg; Sod 384 mg.

Mary F. Evans, West Virginia

CHEESY ZUCCHINI

1 zucchini

1 large tomato

1 large onion

1/4 cup margarine

1/2 teaspoon dillweed

Salt and pepper to taste

1 cup shredded Cheddar cheese

Cut vegetables into thin slices. Sauté in margarine in skillet until tender. Add seasonings and cheese; mix lightly. Simmer, covered, until cheese is melted. Yield: 6 servings.

Approx Per Serving:
Cal 160; Prot 6 g; Carbo 4 g; T Fat 14 g; Chol 20 mg; Potas 160 mg; Sod 209 mg.

Barbara Holmes, Maryland

FRIED APPLES

5 tart apples, peeled, thinly
sliced

1/4 cup melted margarine

1/2 cup sugar

1/4 teaspoon cinnamon

1/4 cup hot water

Place apple slices in melted margarine in skillet. Sprinkle with sugar and cinnamon. Pour hot water carefully down side of skillet. Simmer, covered, for 15 minutes or until apples are tender. Yield: 5 servings.

Approx Per Serving:
Cal 238; Prot 0 g; Carbo 41 g; T Fat 10 g;
Chol 0 mg; Potas 164 mg; Sod 108 mg.

Johnnie Wilcox, Ohio

HONEYED APPLE RINGS

6 medium apples, sliced

1/2 cup honey

2 tablespoons vinegar

1/4 teaspoon salt

1/4 teaspoon cinnamon

Arrange apple slices in 9x13-inch baking dish. Combine honey, vinegar, salt and cinnamon in small bowl. Drizzle over apples. Bake at 325 degrees for 10 to 12 minutes or until tender. Yield: 8 servings.

Approx Per Serving:
Cal 125; Prot 0 g; Carbo 33 g; T Fat 0 g;
Chol 0 mg; Potas 134 mg; Sod 69 mg.

Lori McKinney, Oklahoma

EASY CHEESY MACARONI

1 tablespoon melted butter

1 can Cheddar cheese soup

Salt and pepper to taste

4 cups cooked macaroni

1/2 cup cheese cracker crumbs

Combine butter, soup, salt and pepper in saucepan; mix well. Cook until bubbly. Pour over hot macaroni in serving bowl; toss lightly. Sprinkle with cracker crumbs. Serve immediately. Yield: 6 servings.

Approx Per Serving:
Cal 217; Prot 7 g; Carbo 32 g; T Fat 7 g;
Chol 18 mg; Potas 115 mg; Sod 423 mg.

Margaret Southall, Missouri

Easy Macaroni Bake

1/4 cup finely chopped onion

2 tablespoons butter

1 can tomato soup

1/2 soup can water

3/4 cup shredded process cheese

2 cups cooked macaroni

1/4 cup shredded process cheese

2 tablespoons buttered bread crumbs

Sauté onion in butter in skillet until tender. Stir in soup, water and 3/4 cup cheese. Cook until cheese is melted, stirring frequently. Mix with macaroni in greased baking dish. Top with remaining 1/4 cup cheese and buttered crumbs. Bake at 350 degrees for 20 minutes or until bubbly. Yield: 4 servings.

Approx Per Serving:
Cal 311; Prot 11 g; Carbo 32 g; T Fat 16 g; Chol 43 mg; Potas 262 mg; Sod 991 mg.

Donna Hooper, Louisiana

Baked Pineapple Casserole

1/2 cup margarine, softened

3/4 cup sugar

4 eggs

1 20-ounce can crushed pineapple

5 slices bread, cubed

Cream margarine and sugar in mixer bowl until light and fluffy. Beat in eggs. Add pineapple and bread cubes; mix well. Spoon into greased baking dish. Bake at 350 degrees for 45 minutes or until light brown. Yield: 6 servings.

Approx Per Serving:
Cal 421; Prot 6 g; Carbo 56 g; T Fat 20 g; Chol 183 mg; Potas 176 mg; Sod 346 mg.

Hope E. Morgan, Maryland

Oven Rice

1 small onion, chopped

1 cup rice

1/4 cup butter

1 3-ounce can sliced mushrooms, drained

1 can beef broth

Sauté onion and rice in butter in skillet until golden brown. Add mushrooms. Mix broth with enough water to measure 2 cups. Stir into rice mixture. Pour into greased baking dish. Bake at 350 degrees for 45 minutes, stirring occasionally. Yield: 4 servings.

Approx Per Serving:
Cal 289; Prot 5 g; Carbo 41 g; T Fat 12 g; Chol 31 mg; Potas 159 mg; Sod 421 mg.

Deeann Hairgrove, California

Vegetable Rice

1¹/₃ cups minute rice

1¹/₂ cups cooked mixed vegetables

1¹/₂ cups boiling water

2 tablespoons finely chopped onion

3 tablespoons butter

Salt and pepper to taste

Combine rice and vegetables in boiling water in saucepan. Simmer for 5 minutes. Sauté onion in butter in skillet. Stir into rice mixture. Season to taste. Serve immediately. Yield: 4 servings.

Approx Per Serving:
Cal 236; Prot 4 g; Carbo 35 g; T Fat 9 g;
Chol 23 mg; Potas 183 mg; Sod 97 mg.

Dollye Fineman, Georgia

Cheese Sauce

6 tablespoons butter

6 tablespoons flour

2 cups milk

1 pound Velveeta cheese, cubed

Melt butter in saucepan. Blend in flour. Stir in milk gradually. Cook until thickened, stirring constantly. Add cheese. Cook over low heat until cheese is melted, stirring constantly. Serve over pasta or vegetables. Yield: 10 servings.

Approx Per Serving:
Cal 277; Prot 12 g; Carbo 7 g; T Fat 23 g;
Chol 68 mg; Potas 146 mg; Sod 727 mg.

Naomi Parsons, Arizona

Sweet Pepper Chutney

1 yellow onion, sliced

1 red bell pepper, cut into chunks

1¹/₂ teaspoons chopped jalapeño pepper

1 teaspoon red pepper flakes

¹/₄ teaspoon cloves

2 tablespoons olive oil

1 cup raisins

1   14-ounce can whole tomatoes, drained

¹/₄ cup packed brown sugar

¹/₄ cup lemon juice

Grated rind of 1 lemon

Sauté onion, peppers, red pepper flakes and cloves in 2 tablespoons olive oil in saucepan until onion is transparent. Add raisins, tomatoes, brown sugar, lemon juice and lemon rind. Simmer for 10 minutes. Cool. May store in refrigerator for up to 2 weeks. Serve at room temperature. Yield: 3¹/₂ cups.

Photograph for this recipe is on page 69.

Brisk
Breads

ANGEL BISCUITS

1 package dry yeast
1/2 cup warm water
5 cups flour
3 tablespoons sugar
1 tablespoon baking powder
1 teaspoon soda
1 teaspoon salt
3/4 cup shortening
2 cups buttermilk

Dissolve yeast in warm water. Combine flour, sugar, baking powder, soda and salt in bowl. Cut in shortening until crumbly. Add yeast and buttermilk; mix well. Chill, covered, for up to 3 weeks. Pat desired amount of dough to 3/4-inch thickness on lightly floured surface; cut with biscuit cutter. Place on greased baking sheet. Bake at 400 degrees for 12 minutes.
Yield: 48 servings.

Approx Per Serving:
Cal 84; Prot 2 g; Carbo 11 g; T Fat 3 g;
Chol 0 mg; Potas 31 mg; Sod 93 mg.

Audry Harrison, Virginia

BUTTERMILK BISCUITS

2 cups flour
1 tablespoon baking powder
1/2 teaspoon salt
1/4 teaspoon soda
1/2 cup shortening
3/4 cup buttermilk

Sift dry ingredients into bowl. Cut in shortening until crumbly. Add buttermilk; mix well. Knead 10 to 12 times on lightly floured surface. Pat 1/2 inch thick; cut with biscuit cutter. Place on lightly greased baking sheet. Bake at 450 degrees for 12 minutes or until golden brown. May use additional 2 to 4 tablespoons buttermilk and drop by spoonfuls onto baking sheet. Yield: 12 servings.

Approx Per Serving:
Cal 159; Prot 3 g; Carbo 17 g; T Fat 9 g;
Chol 1 mg; Potas 44 mg; Sod 205 mg.

Mary L. Mingo, Oklahoma

DROP BISCUITS

1 cup self-rising flour
1/2 cup milk
2 tablespoons mayonnaise

Combine flour, milk and mayonnaise in bowl; mix well. Drop by spoonfuls onto greased baking sheet or into greased muffin cups. Bake at 425 degrees until brown. Yield: 6 servings.

Approx Per Serving:
Cal 119; Prot 3 g; Carbo 17 g; T Fat 5 g;
Chol 5 mg; Potas 48 mg; Sod 259 mg.

Callie Wilson, Ohio

Parmesan Biscuits

2 10-count cans refrigerator
 biscuits

1/2 cup melted butter

1 cup Parmesan cheese

Dillweed to taste

Dip each biscuit into melted butter; roll in Parmesan cheese to coat. Place on baking sheet. Sprinkle with dillweed. Bake at 425 degrees until golden brown. Yield: 20 servings.

Approx Per Serving:
Cal 124; Prot 3 g; Carbo 10 g; T Fat 8 g;
Chol 17 mg; Potas 24 mg; Sod 363 mg.

Alpha Lynn Stone, Kansas

Quick Biscuits

1/4 cup sugar

1/3 cup oil

1 egg, beaten

1 package dry yeast

2 cups warm water

4 cups self-rising flour

Combine sugar, oil, egg, yeast and warm water in bowl; mix well. Add flour; mix well. Fill greased muffin cups 3/4 full. Bake at 375 degrees for 20 minutes. May store batter in covered container in refrigerator for up to 2 weeks. Yield: 36 servings.

Approx Per Serving:
Cal 75; Prot 2 g; Carbo 12 g; T Fat 2 g;
Chol 8 mg; Potas 18 mg; Sod 152 mg.

Barbara Gray, West Virginia

Savory Biscuits

1 10-count can refrigerator
 biscuits

1/3 cup melted butter

3 tablespoons crumbled
 bleu cheese

Cut biscuits into quarters. Arrange in 11x17-inch baking pan. Blend butter and bleu cheese in small bowl. Pour over biscuits. Bake at 400 degrees for 15 minutes. Yield: 10 servings.

Approx Per Serving:
Cal 120; Prot 2 g; Carbo 10 g; T Fat 8 g;
Chol 18 mg; Potas 21 mg; Sod 305 mg.

Kay Martin, Georgia

BISCUIT MONKEY BREAD

4 10-count cans refrigerator
biscuits

1¾ cups sugar

1 teaspoon cinnamon

½ cup chopped pecans

1 cup melted margarine

Cut biscuits into quarters. Roll in mixture of sugar and cinnamon. Mix pecans with ¾ of the margarine. Alternate layers of biscuits and pecan mixture in greased tube pan. Bring remaining cinnamon mixture and margarine to a boil in saucepan. Pour over biscuits. Bake at 350 degrees for 25 minutes. Yield: 16 servings.

Approx Per Serving:
Cal 374; Prot 4 g; Carbo 47 g; T Fat 19 g;
Chol 3 mg; Potas 66 mg; Sod 757 mg.

Sandy Randolph, Colorado

QUICK CARAMEL COFFEE RING

¼ cup melted butter

½ cup chopped pecans

¾ cup packed brown sugar

2 tablespoons water

2 10-count cans refrigerator
biscuits

Brush half the butter over bottom and side of bundt pan. Sprinkle with half the pecans. Combine remaining butter, pecans, brown sugar and water in saucepan. Bring to a boil, stirring constantly; remove from heat. Cut biscuits into halves; shape into balls. Alternate layers of biscuits and brown sugar mixture in prepared pan. Bake at 350 degrees for 30 minutes or until brown. Let stand for 2 minutes. Invert onto serving plate. Yield: 8 servings.

Approx Per Serving:
Cal 421; Prot 7 g; Carbo 62 g; T Fat 17 g;
Chol 56 mg; Potas 175 mg; Sod 836 mg.

Joyce Ferguson, Minnesota

BEST CORN BREAD

2 cups buttermilk baking mix

¾ cup yellow cornmeal

¾ cup sugar

½ teaspoon baking powder

1 cup milk

2 eggs, slightly beaten

¾ cup melted butter

Combine baking mix, cornmeal, sugar and baking powder in bowl. Add milk, eggs and butter; mix well. Pour into greased 8x8-inch baking pan. Bake at 350 degrees for 35 to 40 minutes or until brown. Yield: 9 servings.

Approx Per Serving:
Cal 397; Prot 5 g; Carbo 46 g; T Fat 22 g;
Chol 106 mg; Potas 111 mg; Sod 527 mg.

Ruth Diamond, California

BROCCOLI CORN BREAD

1   10-ounce package frozen
    chopped broccoli

1   7-ounce package corn
    bread mix

4 eggs

24 ounces cottage cheese

3/4 cup chopped onion

1/4 cup corn oil

Cook broccoli using package directions; drain well. Combine corn bread mix, eggs, cottage cheese, onion and oil in bowl; mix well. Stir in broccoli. Pour into greased 9x9-inch baking pan. Bake at 350 degrees for 35 minutes or until golden brown. Yield: 9 servings.

Approx Per Serving:
Cal 223; Prot 14 g; Carbo 13 g; T Fat 13 g; Chol 133 mg; Potas 176 mg; Sod 450 mg.

Lisa Boone, Missouri

QUICK CORNMEAL CAKES

1 egg, beaten

1 cup buttermilk

2 tablespoons oil

1/2 cup flour

1/2 cup cornmeal

1 tablespoon sugar

1 teaspoon baking powder

1/2 teaspoon soda

1/2 teaspoon salt

Beat egg with buttermilk and oil in medium bowl. Add flour, cornmeal, sugar, baking powder, soda and salt; mix well. Ladle desired amount of batter onto hot greased griddle. Bake until golden brown on both sides. Serve with butter as for corn bread or with butter and maple syrup as for pancakes.
Yield: 4 servings.

Approx Per Serving:
Cal 238; Prot 7 g; Carbo 32 g; T Fat 9 g; Chol 71 mg; Potas 146 mg; Sod 533 mg.

Kay Campbell, West Virginia

BANANA BREAD

1/2 cup butter, softened

1 cup sugar

2 eggs, beaten

4 medium bananas, mashed

1/4 cup buttermilk

1 teaspoon vanilla extract

2 cups flour

1 teaspoon soda

1 teaspoon baking powder

Cream butter and sugar in mixer bowl until light and fluffy. Add eggs, bananas, buttermilk and vanilla; mix well. Add dry ingredients gradually, mixing well after each addition. Pour into greased and floured 5x9-inch loaf pan. Bake at 350 degrees for 50 minutes or until loaf tests done. Yield: 12 servings.

Approx Per Serving:
Cal 258; Prot 4 g; Carbo 42 g; T Fat 9 g; Chol 67 mg; Potas 192 mg; Sod 178 mg.

Donna Marshall, Iowa

CRANBERRY BANANA BREAD

2/3 cup shortening

1 1/3 cups sugar

3 eggs

2 cups mashed bananas

3 1/2 cups self-rising flour

1/4 teaspoon soda

1 16-ounce can whole
   cranberry sauce

1 cup chopped walnuts

Cream shortening and sugar in mixer bowl until light and fluffy. Beat in eggs and bananas. Add flour and soda; mix well. Mash cranberry sauce with fork. Fold sauce and walnuts into batter. Pour into 2 greased and floured 5x9-inch loaf pans. Bake at 325 degrees for 1 hour or until loaves test done. Yield: 24 servings.

Approx Per Serving:
Cal 244; Prot 3 g; Carbo 37 g; T Fat 10 g;
Chol 34 mg; Potas 129 mg; Sod 220 mg.

Lee Riddle, Texas

RAISIN BREAD

1 cup margarine, softened

2 1/4 cups sugar

3 eggs

1 15-ounce package raisins

6 cups flour

4 teaspoons baking powder

1 1/2 teaspoons cinnamon

2 cups milk

Cream margarine and sugar in bowl until light. Beat in eggs 1 at a time. Toss raisins with 1/2 cup flour. Add remaining flour, baking powder and cinnamon to creamed mixture alternately with milk, mixing well after each addition. Stir in raisins. Pour into 3 greased and floured 5x9-inch loaf pans. Bake at 325 degrees for 1 hour. Yield: 36 servings.

Approx Per Serving:
Cal 220; Prot 4 g; Carbo 39 g; T Fat 6 g;
Chol 25 mg; Potas 136 mg; Sod 110 mg.

Barbara Lewis, Maryland

STRAWBERRY PECAN BREAD

3 cups flour

2 cups sugar

1 tablespoon cinnamon

1 teaspoon soda

1 teaspoon salt

1 cup chopped pecans

2 10-ounce packages frozen
   strawberries, thawed

4 eggs

1 1/4 cups oil

Combine flour, sugar, cinnamon, soda, salt and pecans in bowl; mix well. Add strawberries, eggs and oil; mix well. Pour into 3 greased and floured 5x9-inch loaf pans. Bake at 350 degrees for 1 hour or until loaves test done. Yield: 36 servings.

Approx Per Serving:
Cal 184; Prot 2 g; Carbo 21 g; T Fat 11 g;
Chol 30 mg; Potas 54 mg; Sod 91 mg.

Carolyn Caldwell, Oklahoma

BEER BUNS

3 cups buttermilk baking mix

1/4 cup sugar

1 cup beer

Combine baking mix and sugar in bowl. Add beer; mix with fork until moistened. Spoon into greased muffin cups. Bake at 400 degrees for 20 minutes or until golden brown. Serve hot. Yield: 12 servings.

Approx Per Serving:
Cal 160; Prot 2 g; Carbo 26 g; T Fat 5 g; Chol 0 mg; Potas 51 mg; Sod 398 mg.

Carolyn Merrill, Maryland

APPLESAUCE OAT BRAN MUFFINS

2 egg whites

1 1/4 cups applesauce

1/2 cup raisins

1 cup oat bran

1 cup self-rising flour

1 tablespoon cinnamon

Beat egg whites in small bowl until frothy. Add applesauce and raisins; mix well. Combine oat bran, flour and cinnamon in medium bowl. Add applesauce mixture; mix just until moistened. Fill greased muffin cups 2/3 full. Bake at 400 degrees for 15 minutes or until golden brown. Yield: 10 servings.

Approx Per Serving:
Cal 108; Prot 4 g; Carbo 26 g; T Fat 1 g; Chol 0 mg; Potas 159 mg; Sod 149 mg.

Rikki Larsen, New York

BANANA BRAN MUFFINS

1/4 cup honey

3 egg whites

1/2 cup oil

1/2 cup oat bran

1/2 cup oat flour

3 bananas, mashed

1/2 cup chopped pecans

Combine honey, egg whites and oil in bowl; mix well. Add mixture of oat bran and oat flour alternately with bananas, mixing lightly after each addition. Stir in pecans. Spoon into greased muffin cups. Bake at 350 degrees for 35 minutes. Yield: 12 servings.

Approx Per Serving:
Cal 187; Prot 3 g; Carbo 18 g; T Fat 13 g; Chol 0 mg; Potas 180 mg; Sod 14 mg.

Irlene Carlyle, Alabama

BREADS

BLUEBERRY-ICE CREAM MUFFINS

1 cup self-rising flour

1 cup vanilla ice cream, softened

1 cup blueberries

Combine flour and ice cream in bowl; mix with fork until moistened. Fold in blueberries. Spoon into paper-lined muffin cups. Bake at 350 degrees for 20 minutes or until golden brown. Yield: 12 servings.

Approx Per Serving:
Cal 66; Prot 1 g; Carbo 12 g; T Fat 1 g; Chol 5 mg; Potas 42 mg; Sod 123 mg.

Katie Mosier, Texas

FOOD PROCESSOR BLUEBERRY MUFFINS

1 stick butter, sliced

3/4 cup sugar

2 eggs

1 tablespoon vinegar

1 cup (scant) milk

1 teaspoon soda

2 teaspoons baking powder

2 cups flour

1 1/2 cups blueberries

Process butter, sugar and eggs in food processor for 2 minutes. Combine vinegar, milk and soda. Add to processor. Process for 3 seconds. Add baking powder and flour. Pulse 4 times or just until flour is blended. Stir in blueberries gently by hand. Fill greased muffin cups 1/2 full. Bake at 375 degrees for 25 minutes or until brown. Yield: 24 servings.

Approx Per Serving:
Cal 115; Prot 2 g; Carbo 16 g; T Fat 5 g; Chol 34 mg; Potas 39 mg; Sod 119 mg.

Jamie Morrison, Iowa

CHEESE MUFFINS

1 egg, beaten

3/4 cup milk

1/3 cup oil

1 3/4 cups flour

1/4 cup sugar

2 1/2 teaspoons baking powder

3/4 teaspoon salt

1/2 cup shredded sharp cheese

Beat egg, milk and oil in small bowl. Mix flour, sugar, baking powder, salt and cheese in large bowl. Make well in center. Add egg mixture all at once; stir just until moistened. Batter will be lumpy. Fill greased muffin cups 2/3 full. Bake at 400 degrees for 20 to 25 minutes or until golden brown. Serve hot. Yield: 12 servings.

Approx Per Serving:
Cal 172; Prot 4 g; Carbo 19 g; T Fat 9 g; Chol 28 mg; Potas 50 mg; Sod 248 mg

Gerry Alsop, Oregon

COFFEE CAKE MUFFINS

1/2 cup packed brown sugar
1/2 cup finely chopped pecans
2 teaspoons cinnamon
2 eggs
1/2 cup margarine, softened
1 cup sugar
2 cups sifted flour
1 teaspoon soda
1 teaspoon baking powder
1 teaspoon vanilla extract
1 cup sour cream

Combine brown sugar, pecans and cinnamon in small bowl; mix well. Set aside. Beat eggs, margarine and sugar in bowl until light and fluffy. Add next 3 ingredients; mix well. Add vanilla. Fold in sour cream. Spoon 1/2 of the batter into greased muffin cups; sprinkle with 1/2 of the pecan mixture. Repeat with remaining ingredients. Bake at 350 degrees for 28 minutes. Yield: 20 servings.

Approx Per Serving:
Cal 194; Prot 2 g; Carbo 25 g; T Fat 0 g;
Chol 33 mg; Potas 68 mg; Sod 127 mg.

Bessie Fayette, Florida

MAYONNAISE MUFFINS

2 cups self-rising flour
1/4 cup mayonnaise
1 cup milk
1 tablespoon sugar

Combine flour, mayonnaise, milk and sugar in bowl; mix well. Spoon into greased muffin cups. Bake at 400 degrees for 15 to 20 minutes or until golden brown. Yield: 12 servings.

Approx Per Serving:
Cal 123; Prot 3 g; Carbo 18 g; T Fat 5 g;
Chol 5 mg; Potas 48 mg; Sod 259 mg.

Elise Whitman, California

MUFFIN NUT CUPS

2 cups buttermilk baking mix
1/2 cup sugar
1/4 cup flour
1 egg, beaten
3/4 cup milk
1 cup chopped pecans

Combine baking mix, sugar and flour in bowl. Stir in mixture of egg and milk. Add pecans; mix well. Filled greased and floured 2-inch muffin cups 2/3 full. Bake at 350 degrees until brown. Serve hot or cool. Scoop out centers and fill with chicken salad or other favorite filling. Yield: 18 servings.

Approx Per Serving:
Cal 143; Prot 2 g; Carbo 18 g; T Fat 7 g;
Chol 13 mg; Potas 65 mg; Sod 185 mg.

Ginny Parker, Kentucky

Oatmeal Muffins

1 cup quick-cooking oats

1 cup flour

4 teaspoons baking powder

1/2 teaspoon salt

1/4 cup sugar

1 egg, beaten

1 cup milk

3 tablespoons melted shortening

Combine oats, flour, baking powder, salt and sugar in bowl. Add egg, milk and shortening; mix well. Spoon into greased muffin cups. Bake at 400 degrees for 25 minutes or until brown. Yield: 12 servings.

Approx Per Serving:
Cal 115; Prot 3 g; Carbo 15 g; T Fat 5 g; Chol 26 mg; Potas 55 mg; Sod 245 mg.

Maurine Beller, Ohio

Pear Chocolate Chip Muffins

1 3/4 cups flour

1 cup sugar

2 teaspoons baking powder

1/4 teaspoon salt

2 eggs, slightly beaten

1 cup sour cream

1/4 cup melted butter

1 teaspoon vanilla extract

1 1/2 cups chopped pears

1 cup miniature chocolate chips

1/4 cup chopped walnuts

1/4 cup sugar

2 tablespoons butter, softened

Combine flour, 1 cup sugar, baking powder and salt in mixer bowl. Mix eggs, sour cream, 1/4 cup butter, vanilla, pears and chocolate chips in bowl. Add to dry ingredients; mix just until moistened. Fill 12 greased muffin cups 3/4 full. Mix walnuts, 1/4 cup sugar and 2 tablespoons butter in bowl until crumbly. Sprinkle over muffins. Bake at 400 degrees for 18 to 20 minutes or until muffins test done. Yield: 12 servings.

Photograph for this recipe is on page 103.

Whole Wheat Yogurt Muffins

1 cup whole wheat flour

3/4 cup all-purpose flour

1/3 cup sugar

1/4 teaspoon salt

1/2 teaspoon soda

1/2 cup butter

1 egg

1 cup fruit-flavored yogurt

Combine flours, sugar, salt and soda in bowl. Cut in butter until crumbly. Add egg and yogurt; mix just until moistened. Spoon into greased muffin cups. Bake at 375 degrees for 20 minutes or until brown. Yield: 12 servings.

Approx Per Serving:
Cal 177; Prot 4 g; Carbo 22 g; T Fat 9 g; Chol 44 mg; Potas 89 mg; Sod 160 mg.

Amy Weaver, California

HUNGRY FAMILY SUPPERS

Satisfy everyone including the cook.

Lazy Stew, 48

Green Bean Salad, 39

Quick Cornmeal Cakes, 97

Pantry Shelf Chocolate Cake, 125

Microwave Apricot Chicken, 61

Golden Garden Rice Salad, 38

Easy Popovers, 105

Quick Key Lime Pie, 148

EASY POPOVERS

6 eggs
1/4 cup oil
2 cups milk
1 3/4 cups flour
1 teaspoon salt

Beat eggs and oil in bowl. Add milk, flour and salt; beat until smooth. Spoon into greased muffin cups. Bake at 375 degrees for 25 minutes or until firm and brown. Serve immediately. Yield: 20 servings.

Approx Per Serving:
Cal 103; Prot 4 g; Carbo 10 g; T Fat 5 g; Chol 86 mg; Potas 63 mg; Sod 138 mg.

Joan Freeman, California

GINGERBREAD PANCAKES

1 egg, beaten
1 cup milk
1   14-ounce package gingerbread mix
2 tablespoons melted butter

Beat egg and milk in bowl. Add gingerbread mix and butter; mix well. Drop 2 or 3 tablespoonfuls per pancake onto hot lightly greased griddle. Bake until brown on both sides. Serve with honey or syrup. Yield: 20 servings.

Approx Per Serving:
Cal 96; Prot 1 g; Carbo 15 g; T Fat 3 g; Chol 5 mg; Potas 95 mg; Sod 101 mg.

Marnie Wallace, West Virginia

OVEN PANCAKE

6 eggs
1 cup milk
1 cup flour
1 teaspoon salt
1/2 cup margarine

Combine eggs and milk in mixer bowl. Beat for 3 minutes. Sift in flour and salt. Beat for 3 minutes longer. Melt margarine in 9x13-inch baking pan in 425-degree oven. Pour batter into prepared pan. Bake for 20 to 25 minutes or until puffed and golden brown. Cut into squares. Serve with butter and syrup or sweetened fresh fruit. Yield: 10 servings.

Approx Per Serving:
Cal 189; Prot 6 g; Carbo 11 g; T Fat 13 g; Chol 168 mg; Potas 88 mg; Sod 372 mg.

Karen Shaw, Kentucky

SCRUMPTIOUS OATMEAL PANCAKES

1 cup flour
4 teaspoons baking powder
1 teaspoon salt
1 cup quick-cooking oats
1 egg, beaten
2 cups milk
2 tablespoons oil

Sift flour, baking powder and salt into bowl. Add oats. Beat egg with milk and oil. Add to oats mixture; mix well. Ladle desired amount of batter onto hot greased griddle. Bake until golden brown on both sides. Serve with butter and syrup. May substitute cornmeal for oats. Yield: 6 servings.

Approx Per Serving:
Cal 206; Prot 7 g; Carbo 24 g; T Fat 9 g;
Chol 57 mg; Potas 165 mg; Sod 684 mg.

Millie Foster, Arkansas

SEVEN-UP PANCAKES

1 egg, well beaten
1 tablespoon melted shortening
10 tablespoons 7-Up
1 cup buttermilk pancake mix.

Combine egg and shortening in bowl. Stir in 6 tablespoons 7-Up. Add pancake mix; blend well. Stir in remaining 7-Up. Spoon onto hot greased griddle. Bake until brown on both sides. Yield: 2 servings.

Approx Per Serving:
Cal 380; Prot 9 g; Carbo 60 g; T Fat 11 g;
Chol 126 mg; Potas 142 mg; Sod 996 mg.

Pauline Polk, Indiana

ORANGE FRENCH TOAST

1/4 cup margarine
1/3 cup sugar
1/4 teaspoon cinnamon
1 teaspoon grated orange rind
2/3 cup orange juice
4 eggs, slightly beaten
8 slices bread
1/2 cup chopped pecans

Melt margarine with sugar and cinnamon in saucepan. Pour into 9x13-inch baking dish. Mix orange rind, orange juice and eggs in bowl. Dip bread into egg mixture; arrange in baking dish. Pour remaining egg mixture over bread. Sprinkle with pecans. Bake at 350 degrees until golden brown. Yield: 4 servings.

Approx Per Serving:
Cal 256; Prot 6 g; Carbo 26 g; T Fat 15 g;
Chol 106 mg; Potas 138 mg; Sod 246 mg.

Luanne Roberts, Tennessee

WAFFLES

| 2 cups buttermilk baking mix |
| 1 egg |
| 1/2 cup oil |
| 1 1/3 cups club soda |

Combine baking mix, egg, oil and club soda in bowl; mix well. Bake in hot waffle iron according to manufacturer's instructions. Serve with butter and syrup. Yield: 8 servings.

Approx Per Serving:
Cal 266; Prot 3 g; Carbo 21 g; T Fat 19 g;
Chol 34 mg; Potas 54 mg; Sod 414 mg.

Callie Howard, New Jersey

CROCK•POT HONEY-WHEAT BREAD

| 2 cups milk, scalded |
| 2 tablespoons oil |
| 1/4 cup honey |
| 3/4 teaspoon salt |
| 1 package dry yeast |
| 3 cups whole wheat flour |

Preheat Crock•Pot on High for 30 minutes. Cool milk to lukewarm. Combine milk, oil, honey, salt, yeast and 1/2 of the flour in mixer bowl. Beat for 2 minutes. Mix in remaining flour. Pour into greased 3-pound coffee can. Let stand for 5 minutes. Place in Crock•Pot. Cook on High for 2 to 3 hours or until loaf tests done. Remove from Crock•Pot. Let stand for 5 to 10 minutes. Remove from can. Serve warm. Yield: 15 servings.

Approx Per Serving:
Cal 135; Prot 4 g; Carbo 23 g; T Fat 3 g;
Chol 4 mg; Potas 145 mg; Sod 121 mg.

Mary Ann Summers, Illinois

PIZZA BREAD

| 3 cups flour |
| 1 package dry yeast |
| 1 teaspoon oregano |
| 1 teaspoon garlic salt |
| 2 tablespoons melted butter |
| 1 tablespoon sugar |
| 1/4 cup finely chopped pepperoni |
| 1 1/4 cups warm water |

Combine flour, yeast, oregano, garlic salt, butter, sugar and pepperoni in bowl; mix well. Add water; mix well with wooden spoon. Pour into greased 5x9-inch loaf pan. Let rise for 30 minutes. Bake at 375 degrees for 35 minutes or until golden brown. Serve warm or cool and slice for grilled cheese sandwiches.
Yield: 12 servings.

Approx Per Serving:
Cal 148; Prot 4 g; Carbo 25 g; T Fat 3 g;
Chol 6 mg; Potas 50 mg; Sod 243 mg.

Peggy McIntire, Minnesota

SIXTY-MINUTE ROLLS

2 packages dry yeast

2 tablespoons sugar

1 teaspoon salt

3 cups flour

1½ cups milk

3 tablespoons margarine

1 cup flour

Combine yeast, sugar, salt and 3 cups flour in bowl. Heat milk with margarine in saucepan just until margarine begins to melt. Add to flour mixture; mix well. Stir in remaining 1 cup flour. Let rise, covered, for 15 minutes. Spoon into greased muffin cups. Let rise for 15 minutes longer. Bake at 400 degrees for 10 minutes or until brown. Yield: 20 servings.

Approx Per Serving:
Cal 124; Prot 4 g; Carbo 21 g; T Fat 3 g; Chol 2 mg; Potas 63 mg; Sod 135 mg.

Sarah Linn, Colorado

CARAMEL PLUCK-IT CAKE

3 10-count cans refrigerator buttermilk biscuits

¾ cup sugar

1 tablespoon cinnamon

1 cup packed brown sugar

½ cup margarine

Cut biscuits into quarters. Coat with mixture of sugar and cinnamon. Place in greased bundt pan. Sprinkle with any remaining cinnamon-sugar. Melt brown sugar and margarine in saucepan. Pour over biscuits. Place in cold oven. Bake at 350 degrees for 35 minutes or until brown. Invert onto serving plate. Let stand for 5 to 10 minutes; remove pan. Yield: 16 servings.

Approx Per Serving:
Cal 262; Prot 3 g; Carbo 41 g; T Fat 10 g; Chol 2 mg; Potas 86 mg; Sod 540 mg.

Karen Reiersen, Indiana

STICKY BUNS

24 brown and serve rolls

½ cup sugar

2 tablespoons cinnamon

1 cup pecans

1 cup coconut

1 cup light corn syrup

¾ cup melted butter

Cut rolls into halves. Combine sugar, cinnamon, pecans, coconut and corn syrup in bowl; mix well. Spread evenly on baking sheet lined with foil. Dip roll halves into melted butter. Place cut side down on prepared baking sheet. Pour remaining butter over rolls. Bake at 350 degrees for 10 to 15 minutes. Yield: 24 servings.

Approx Per Serving:
Cal 225; Prot 3 g; Carbo 29 g; T Fat 11 g; Chol 19 mg; Potas 76 mg; Sod 222 mg.

Eloise Dunsmore, Mississippi

CHEESE BREAD

2 cups shredded Cheddar
cheese

1/4 cup mayonnaise

1 tablespoon grated onion

2 tablespoons butter, softened

Cayenne pepper to taste

1   16-ounce loaf French bread,
sliced

Combine cheese, mayonnaise, onion, butter and cayenne pepper in bowl; mix well. Spread on bread slices; arrange on baking sheet. Bake at 350 degrees for 10 minutes or until bubbly and golden brown. Yield: 12 servings.

Approx Per Serving:
Cal 234; Prot 8 g; Carbo 20 g; T Fat 13 g;
Chol 28 mg; Potas 57 mg; Sod 378 mg.

Louise Blufeld, Missouri

CHEESY GARLIC BREAD

1 cup shredded mozzarella
cheese

3/4 cup margarine, softened

1/3 cup finely chopped onion

2 tablespoons parsley flakes

1   16-ounce loaf French bread,
sliced

Garlic salt to taste

Combine cheese, margarine, onion and parsley in bowl; mix well. Spread on bread slices; sprinkle with garlic salt. Reassemble slices into loaf; wrap in foil. Bake at 375 degrees for 15 minutes. Yield: 12 servings.

Approx Per Serving:
Cal 238; Prot 6 g; Carbo 20 g; T Fat 15 g;
Chol 7 mg; Potas 57 mg; Sod 389 mg.

Jan Lake, North Dakota

HERB AND CHEESE BREAD

1 cup margarine, softened

1 teaspoon prepared mustard

2 teaspoons lemon juice

1 teaspoon Beau Monde
seasoning

2 tablespoons grated onion

1   16-ounce loaf French bread

4 ounces Swiss cheese, thinly
sliced

Combine margarine, mustard, lemon juice, seasoning and onion in bowl; mix well. Cut loaf into 1/2-inch slices to but not through bottom. Spread cut surfaces with margarine mixture. Place cheese between slices. Wrap in foil. Bake at 325 degrees for 25 minutes.
Yield: 12 servings.

Approx Per Serving:
Cal 281; Prot 6 g; Carbo 20 g; T Fat 19 g;
Chol 9 mg; Potas 57 mg; Sod 428 mg.

Adelaide Foreman, Michigan

COCONUT TOASTIES

8 slices bread

1/4 cup butter, softened

1/2 cup packed brown sugar

1/2 cup flaked coconut

Cut bread into strips. Cream butter and brown sugar in bowl. Spread over bread strips; sprinkle with coconut. Place on lightly greased baking sheet. Broil until light brown. Yield: 8 servings.

Approx Per Serving:
Cal 198; Prot 3 g; Carbo 29 g; T Fat 8 g; Chol 16 mg; Potas 96 mg; Sod 199 mg.

Helen Calhoun, Nebraska

QUICK BREADSTICKS

12 hot dog buns

1 cup butter, softened

1 teaspoon basil

1/4 teaspoon garlic powder

Cut buns into quarters lengthwise. Blend butter, basil and garlic powder in small bowl. Spread on buns; place on baking sheet. Bake at 250 degrees for 1 1/2 hours or until crisp. Yield: 48 servings.

Approx Per Serving:
Cal 63; Prot 1 g; Carbo 5 g; T Fat 4 g; Chol 10 mg; Potas 15 mg; Sod 93 mg.

Maxine Brown, Kansas

HERB ROLLS

1/4 cup melted margarine

1 1/2 teaspoons minced parsley

3 tablespoons Parmesan cheese

1/2 teaspoon dillseed

1   10-count can refrigerator buttermilk biscuits

Combine margarine, parsley, cheese and dillseed in 9-inch baking pan. Cut biscuits into halves. Arrange biscuits in pan, turning to coat with butter mixture. Bake at 425 degrees for 12 to 15 minutes. Yield: 20 servings.

Approx Per Serving:
Cal 57; Prot 1 g; Carbo 5 g; T Fat 4 g; Chol 1 mg; Potas 12 mg; Sod 165 mg.

Barbara Bascom, North Carolina

Dazzling Desserts

AMBROSIA PARFAITS

1 8-ounce can mandarin
   oranges, drained

¼ cup chopped toasted
   blanched almonds

2 cups whipped topping

1 4-ounce package toasted
coconut instant pudding mix

2 cups milk

Reserve 5 orange sections. Fold remaining oranges and almonds into whipped topping in bowl. Combine pudding mix and milk in mixer bowl. Beat slowly for 2 minutes. Alternate layers of whipped topping mixture and pudding in parfait glasses until all ingredients are used. Chill until serving time. Garnish with reserved orange sections and mint sprigs. Yield: 5 servings.

Approx Per Serving:
Cal 310; Prot 5 g; Carbo 42 g; T Fat 15 g; Chol 13 mg; Potas 227 mg; Sod 204 mg.

Marie Cook, Illinois

ANGEL FOOD AND PEANUT BRITTLE DESSERT

1 angel food cake

2 cups whipping cream

2 tablespoons confectioners'
sugar

1 cup crushed peanut brittle

Split cake horizontally into 2 layers. Combine whipping cream and confectioners' sugar in mixer bowl; beat until soft peaks form. Fold in peanut brittle. Spread between layers and over top and side of cake. Store in refrigerator until serving time. Yield: 12 servings.

Approx Per Serving:
Cal 306; Prot 5 g; Carbo 38 g; T Fat 16 g; Chol 54 mg; Potas 115 mg; Sod 287 mg.

Helen Wenger, California

EASY BAKED APPLES

6 baking apples

¾ cup honey

2 tablespoons lemon juice

Core apples; peel top third of each. Place apples in shallow baking dish. Add water to cover bottom of dish. Blend honey and lemon juice in bowl. Brush over apples. Pour remaining honey mixture into apple centers. Bake at 350 degrees for 45 minutes or until tender, basting occasionally with pan juices. Yield: 6 servings.

Approx Per Serving:
Cal 209; Prot 0 g; Carbo 56 g; T Fat 3 g; Chol 0 mg; Potas 181 mg; Sod 3 mg.

Regina Carson, Alabama

SPICY APPLE CRISP

1 21-ounce can apple
    pie filling

1 cup quick-cooking oats

1/4 cup butter, softened

1/2 cup packed brown sugar

1 teaspoon cinnamon

1/2 teaspoon nutmeg

Spread pie filling in loaf pan. Mix oats, butter, brown sugar, cinnamon and nutmeg in small bowl. Sprinkle over pie filling. Bake at 325 degrees for 30 minutes. Serve with vanilla ice cream. Yield: 4 servings.

Approx Per Serving:
Cal 380; Prot 2 g; Carbo 70 g; T Fat 12 g; Chol 31 mg; Potas 249 mg; Sod 248 mg.

Lorene Leebrick, Tennessee

APPLE CRUNCH

6 cups sliced peeled tart apples

1/2 cup sifted flour

1/4 teaspoon cinnamon

1 cup packed brown sugar

3/4 cup butter

1 1/4 cups oats

1/4 cup chopped walnuts

Place apples in greased 8x8-inch baking dish. Mix flour, cinnamon and brown sugar in small bowl. Cut in butter until crumbly. Stir in oats and walnuts. Sprinkle over apples. Bake at 350 degrees for 50 to 60 minutes or until apples are tender. Serve with ice cream or maple syrup. Yield: 8 servings.

Approx Per Serving:
Cal 404; Prot 4 g; Carbo 54 g; T Fat 21 g; Chol 47 mg; Potas 265 mg; Sod 158 mg.

Bev Cooke, Texas

MICROWAVE APPLE TOPPING FOR ICE CREAM

1 21-ounce can apple
    pie filling

1 2-layer package white
    cake mix

3 tablespoons margarine

1/3 cup packed light brown
    sugar

Spoon pie filling into 8x8-inch glass baking dish. Sprinkle cake mix over filling; dot with margarine. Sprinkle brown sugar over top. Microwave on High for 12 minutes. Let stand for 5 minutes. Serve warm over ice cream. Yield: 12 servings.

Approx Per Serving:
Cal 277; Prot 2 g; Carbo 54 g; T Fat 6 g; Chol 0 mg; Potas 62 mg; Sod 939 mg.

Carol Furey, Florida

No-Bake Blueberry Cheesecake

4 ounces fine graham cracker crumbs

1/2 cup melted butter

1/2 cup sugar

2 envelopes whipped topping mix

16 ounces cream cheese, softened

1 cup sugar

1 21-ounce can blueberry pie filling

Combine crumbs, butter and 1/2 cup sugar in bowl; mix well. Press over bottom of 9x13-inch dish. Prepare whipped topping mix using package directions. Beat cream cheese with 1 cup sugar in mixer bowl until light and fluffy. Fold into whipped topping. Spoon into prepared dish. Chill until firm. Top with pie filling. Chill until serving time. Yield: 12 servings.

Approx Per Serving:
Cal 401; Prot 4 g; Carbo 47 g; T Fat 23 g; Chol 63 mg; Potas 126 mg; Sod 256 mg.

Debbie Sherman, California

Miniature Cheesecakes

9 ounces cream cheese, softened

1 cup sugar

5 eggs

1 1/2 teaspoons vanilla extract

1 1/2 cups sour cream

1/2 cup sugar

1/2 teaspoon vanilla extract

Combine cream cheese and 1 cup sugar in bowl; mix well. Add eggs and 1 1/2 teaspoons vanilla; beat well. Fill paper-lined muffin cups 2/3 full. Bake at 300 degrees for 30 minutes. Mix sour cream, 1/2 cup sugar and 1/2 teaspoon vanilla in bowl. Place 1 teaspoonful in each muffin cup. Bake for 5 to 10 minutes longer.
Yield: 12 servings.

Approx Per Serving:
Cal 265; Prot 5 g; Carbo 27 g; T Fat 16 g; Chol 125 mg; Potas 95 mg; Sod 108 mg.

Charlene Mason, Nebraska

Cherry Crisp

2 21-ounce cans cherry pie filling

1 2-layer package yellow cake mix

3/4 cup melted margarine

3/4 cup chopped pecans

Spoon pie filling into greased 10x14-inch baking dish. Sprinkle with cake mix. Drizzle with margarine; sprinkle with pecans. Bake at 325 degrees for 40 to 45 minutes or until brown and crisp. Yield: 15 servings.

Approx Per Serving:
Cal 343; Prot 2 g; Carbo 50 g; T Fat 16 g; Chol 0 mg; Potas 91 mg; Sod 340 mg.

Joan Leebrick, Tennessee

Easy Cherry Dessert

2 21-ounce cans cherry
   pie filling

1 2-layer package white
   cake mix

½ cup melted butter

Spoon pie filling into 9x13-inch baking pan. Sprinkle cake mix over top. Drizzle with butter. Bake at 375 degrees for 25 minutes or until golden brown. Yield: 12 servings.

Approx Per Serving:
Cal 345; Prot 2 g; Carbo 61 g; T Fat 11 g;
Chol 21 mg; Potas 81 mg; Sod 356 mg.

Doris Williams, Illinois

Cherry-Pineapple Delight

1 21-ounce can cherry
   pie filling

1 8-ounce can crushed
   pineapple

1 2-layer package yellow
   cake mix

1 cup melted margarine

2 cups chopped pecans

Combine pie filling and pineapple in bowl; mix well. Spoon into buttered 9x13-inch baking pan. Sprinkle with cake mix; drizzle with margarine. Top with pecans. Bake at 350 degrees for 40 minutes. Yield: 12 servings.

Approx Per Serving:
Cal 513; Prot 4 g; Carbo 56 g; T Fat 32 g;
Chol 0 mg; Potas 144 mg; Sod 456 mg.

Ruth Phillips, Arizona

Chocoberry Cooler

¾ cup milk

¼ cup sweetened fresh
strawberries

2 tablespoons chocolate syrup

2 tablespoons vanilla ice cream

2 small scoops vanilla ice cream

Chilled ginger ale

Combine milk, strawberries, chocolate syrup and 2 tablespoons ice cream in blender container. Process until smooth. Alternate scoops of ice cream and purée in tall glass. Fill glass with ginger ale. Garnish with fresh strawberry and mint leaves. Serve immediately.
Yield: 1 serving.

Photograph for this recipe is on page 17.

MICROWAVE CHOCOLATE FONDUE

1   14-ounce can sweetened condensed milk
10 ounces marshmallow creme
1/2 cup milk
1 teaspoon vanilla extract
2 cups semisweet chocolate chips

Combine sweetened condensed milk, marshmallow creme, milk, vanilla and chocolate chips in glass bowl; mix well. Microwave on Medium for 4 minutes or until chocolate chips soften. Beat until smooth and creamy. Serve warm with cake cubes, fruit and marshmallows for dipping. Yield: 20 servings.

Approx Per Serving:
Cal 198; Prot 3 g; Carbo 32 g; T Fat 8 g;
Chol 8 mg; Potas 146 mg; Sod 39 mg.

Kay Lee, California

BLENDER EGG CUSTARD

3 eggs
1   12-ounce can evaporated milk
1 cup sugar
3 tablespoons flour
3 tablespoons melted butter
1/4 teaspoon nutmeg
1/4 teaspoon vanilla extract

Combine eggs, evaporated milk, sugar, flour, butter, nutmeg and vanilla in blender container. Process until smooth. Pour into greased and floured glass pie plate. Bake at 350 degrees until set and light brown. Yield: 8 servings.

Approx Per Serving:
Cal 232; Prot 6 g; Carbo 32 g; T Fat 10 g;
Chol 104 mg; Potas 158 mg; Sod 108 mg.

Lois Berman, Illinois

CHILLED FRUIT BOWL

1   29-ounce can pineapple chunks
1   29-ounce can peaches, drained
1   29-ounce can fruit cocktail, drained
3 bananas, sliced
2 tablespoons instant orange breakfast drink mix
1   4-ounce package vanilla instant pudding mix

Combine undrained pineapple, peaches, fruit cocktail and bananas in bowl; mix gently. Stir in dry breakfast drink mix and pudding mix. Chill until serving time. Yield: 16 servings.

Approx Per Serving:
Cal 144; Prot 1 g; Carbo 37 g; T Fat 0 g;
Chol 0 mg; Potas 235 mg; Sod 54 mg.

Eura Sherman, Arkansas

CURRIED FRUIT

1	20-ounce can peaches
1	20-ounce can pears
1	20-ounce can pineapple
	1/2 cup butter
	1 cup packed brown sugar
	1 tablespoon curry powder
	1/4 teaspoon salt

Drain fruit; place in baking dish. Heat butter, brown sugar, curry powder and salt in saucepan until sugar dissolves. Pour over fruit. Bake at 350 degrees for 30 minutes.
Yield:10 servings.

Approx Per Serving:
Cal 291; Prot 1 g; Carbo 55 g; T Fat 9 g; Chol 25 mg; Potas 227 mg; Sod 148 mg.

Alma Parsons, Oklahoma

FRUIT FLUFF

	8 ounces cream cheese, softened
	2 cups milk
1	4-ounce package vanilla instant pudding mix
1	11-ounce can mandarin oranges, drained
1	16-ounce can pineapple chunks, drained
	1 cup miniature marshmallows

Blend cream cheese and 1/2 cup milk in mixer bowl until light and fluffy. Add remaining milk and pudding mix; mix well. Stir in oranges, pineapple and marshmallows. Chill until serving time. Yield: 12 servings.

Approx Per Serving:
Cal 176; Prot 3 g; Carbo 24 g; T Fat 8 g; Chol 26 mg; Potas 138 mg; Sod 142 mg.

Sandra Boyd, Tennessee

FRUIT KABOBS

	4 apples
1	11-ounce can mandarin oranges
	12 apricot halves
	12 dried prunes
	6 canned green figs, drained
	1 1/2 cups orange marmalade

Slice each apple into 6 wedges. Drain oranges, reserving juice. Thread fruits onto 6 skewers in order listed. Thin marmalade to desired consistency using reserved orange juice. Dip kabobs in marmalade mixture. Place on rack in broiler pan. Broil for 3 to 8 minutes or to desired degree of doneness. Serve hot. Yield: 6 servings.

Approx Per Serving:
Cal 376; Prot 2 g; Carbo 99 g; T Fat 1 g; Chol 0 mg; Potas 896 mg; Sod 21 mg.

Dianah Sue Ratliff, Oklahoma

DESSERTS

HEAVENLY HASH

8 ounces cream cheese, softened
16 ounces whipped topping
2 20-ounce cans crushed pineapple
2 11-ounce cans mandarin oranges, drained
2 cups miniature marshmallows
1 cup chopped pecans

Combine cream cheese and whipped topping in bowl; mix until smooth. Drain pineapple, reserving 1/2 cup juice. Add pineapple, oranges and marshmallows to whipped topping mixture; mix well. Stir in pecans and reserved juice. Yield: 15 servings.

Approx Per Serving:
Cal 291; Prot 3 g; Carbo 32 g; T Fat 18 g; Chol 17 mg; Potas 168 mg; Sod 63 mg.

Katrina C. Moran, Tennessee

MIXED FRUIT DELIGHT

2 cups whipping cream, whipped
1/4 cup sugar
2 tablespoons mayonnaise
2 29-ounce cans fruit cocktail, drained
1 8-ounce can crushed pineapple, drained
1 cup chopped pecans
2 cups miniature marshmallows

Blend whipped cream, sugar and mayonnaise in large bowl. Fold in fruit, pecans and marshmallows. Chill until serving time. Yield: 15 servings.

Approx Per Serving:
Cal 301; Prot 2 g; Carbo 35 g; T Fat 19 g; Chol 45 mg; Potas 165 mg; Sod 36 mg.

Caren Hunt, New York

ICE CREAM CRUNCH

2 tablespoons melted butter
1 cup coarsely crushed rice cereal
1/2 cup chopped walnuts
1 quart vanilla ice cream, softened

Combine butter, cereal and walnuts in bowl; mix well. Spread on baking sheet. Bake at 350 degrees for 12 minutes or until golden brown; cool. Layer half the cereal mixture, all the ice cream and remaining cereal in 7x11-inch dish. Freeze until firm. Yield: 8 servings.

Approx Per Serving:
Cal 246; Prot 4 g; Carbo 26 g; T Fat 15 g; Chol 37 mg; Potas 178 mg; Sod 162 mg.

Betty H. Long, Maryland

LEMON DELIGHT

1 small package lemon instant pudding mix

1 6-ounce can crushed pineapple, drained

1 angel food cake

Prepare pudding using package directions. Stir in pineapple. Tear cake into bite-sized pieces. Fold into pineapple mixture. Spoon into shallow dish. Chill overnight. Yield: 8 servings.

Approx Per Serving:
Cal 291; Prot 7 g; Carbo 60 g; T Fat 2 g;
Chol 8 mg; Potas 185 mg; Sod 539 mg.

Joan Dennis, Virginia

MALLOW SAUCE

1 7-ounce jar marshmallow creme

3 ounces cream cheese, softened

Combine marshmallow creme and cream cheese in blender container. Process until smooth. Serve over chocolate, lemon or pound cake or over bread pudding. May serve as dip with assorted bite-sized fresh fruit.
Yield: 10 servings.

Approx Per Serving:
Cal 115; Prot 1 g; Carbo 20 g; T Fat 4 g;
Chol 12 mg; Potas 21 mg; Sod 46 mg.

Henrietta Ivers, New Jersey

OREO COOKIE DELIGHT

1½ cups Oreo cookie crumbs

3 tablespoons melted butter

½ gallon vanilla ice cream, softened

1 8-ounce jar fudge ice cream topping

½ cup chopped pecans

12 ounces whipped topping

1 cup Oreo cookie crumbs

Mix 1½ cups cookie crumbs with butter in bowl. Press into 9x13-inch dish. Layer ice cream, fudge topping, pecans and whipped topping in prepared dish. Sprinkle with remaining 1 cup cookie crumbs. Freeze until serving time. Yield: 16 servings.

Approx Per Serving:
Cal 495; Prot 6 g; Carbo 59 g; T Fat 27 g;
Chol 35 mg; Potas 246 mg; Sod 292 mg.

Jennifer Planer, Iowa

PEACH COBBLER

½ cup butter

1 cup milk

¾ cup buttermilk baking mix

1 cup sugar

1   28-ounce can peaches

Melt butter in 9x13-inch baking dish. Mix milk, baking mix and sugar in bowl. Pour into prepared dish. Drain peaches, reserving ½ cup juice. Spoon peaches over batter. Drizzle with reserved juice. Bake at 350 degrees until golden brown. Yield: 6 servings.

Approx Per Serving:
Cal 455; Prot 3 g; Carbo 72 g; T Fat 19 g; Chol 47 mg; Potas 205 mg; Sod 354 mg.

Betty McGinty, Missouri

EASY PEACH COBBLER

1   29-ounce can sliced peaches

1   2-layer package yellow cake mix

1 stick margarine, sliced

Pour undrained peaches into buttered 9x13-inch baking dish. Sprinkle cake mix over top. Dot with margarine. Bake at 350 degrees for 35 to 40 minutes or until light brown. Serve warm with ice cream. Yield: 10 servings.

Approx Per Serving:
Cal 362; Prot 3 g; Carbo 59 g; T Fat 13 g; Chol 0 mg; Potas 80 mg; Sod 426 mg.

Donna C. Stanton, Maryland

PEACH CRISP

1   28-ounce can sliced peaches

1   2-layer package butter brickle cake mix

1 cup coconut

1 cup chopped pecans

½ cup melted margarine

Pour undrained peaches into 9x13-inch baking pan. Sprinkle with cake mix; top with mixture of coconut and pecans. Drizzle with margarine. Bake at 325 degrees for 50 to 55 minutes or until brown. Serve with ice cream or whipped topping. Yield: 12 servings.

Approx Per Serving:
Cal 395; Prot 3 g; Carbo 54 g; T Fat 20 g; Chol 0 mg; Potas 123 mg; Sod 371 mg.

Dorothy Bobbitt, Oklahoma

PECAN DESSERT

1 roll refrigerator sugar cookie dough
1   4-ounce package butterscotch instant pudding mix
³/₄ cup dark corn syrup
²/₃ cup milk
1 egg
1¹/₂ cups pecan halves

Slice cookie dough ¹/₄ inch thick. Press slices over bottom and ³/₄ inch up sides of 9x13-inch baking pan. Mix pudding mix, corn syrup, milk and egg in bowl. Stir in pecans. Spoon into prepared pan. Bake at 350 degrees for 30 to 35 minutes or until filling is set. Cool completely. Cut into squares. Serve with ice cream. Yield: 12 servings.

Approx Per Serving:
Cal 321; Prot 3 g; Carbo 44 g; T Fat 17 g; Chol 36 mg; Potas 114 mg; Sod 175 mg.

Martha Brice, Florida

HEAVENLY BANANA PUDDING

2   4-ounce packages vanilla instant pudding mix
3 cups milk
8 ounces whipped topping
1 cup sour cream
2   12-ounce packages vanilla wafers
6 large bananas, sliced

Combine pudding mix, milk, whipped topping and sour cream in bowl; mix gently. Crush and reserve several vanilla wafers. Alternate layers of remaining wafers, pudding and bananas in 9x13-inch dish, ending with pudding. Sprinkle with reserved crumbs. Chill until serving time. Yield: 20 servings.

Approx Per Serving:
Cal 314; Prot 4 g; Carbo 48 g; T Fat 13 g; Chol 31 mg; Potas 246 mg; Sod 228 mg.

Donna Brown, Kansas

CHOCOLATE BANANA PUDDING

3   12-ounce packages vanilla wafers
1   6-ounce package chocolate instant pudding mix
1   6-ounce package vanilla instant pudding mix
6 cups milk
6 bananas, sliced

Line bottom and side of large bowl with vanilla wafers. Prepare each pudding mix according to package directions, using 3 cups of milk with each mix. Layer half the bananas, chocolate pudding, vanilla wafers, remaining bananas and vanilla pudding in prepared bowl. Chill until serving time. Yield: 20 servings.

Approx Per Serving:
Cal 375; Prot 5 g; Carbo 64 g; T Fat 12 g; Chol 42 mg; Potas 298 mg; Sod 336 mg.

Donna Barnes, Ohio

Banana Pudding

2 3-ounce packages banana instant pudding mix

3 cups cold milk

1 14-ounce can sweetened condensed milk

12 ounces whipped topping

1 16-ounce package vanilla wafers

5 medium bananas, sliced

Prepare pudding according to package directions, using 3 cups milk. Fold in sweetened condensed milk and 1 cup whipped topping. Layer vanilla wafers, bananas and pudding mixture 1/2 at a time in 9x13-inch dish. Top with remaining whipped topping. Chill, covered, until serving time. Yield: 16 servings.

Approx Per Serving:
Cal 379; Prot 6 g; Carbo 59 g; T Fat 14 g; Chol 32 mg; Potas 334 mg; Sod 234 mg.

Marie E. Rice, Alabama

Quick Rice Pudding

1 cup minute rice

1 cup water

3 tablespoons raisins

1/4 teaspoon salt

1 4-ounce package vanilla instant pudding mix

1/8 teaspoon cinnamon

Combine rice, water, raisins and salt in saucepan. Bring to a boil; let stand until cool. Prepare pudding using package directions. Stir in rice mixture and cinnamon. Chill until serving time. Yield: 4 servings.

Approx Per Serving:
Cal 231; Prot 4 g; Carbo 47 g; T Fat 2 g; Chol 8 mg; Potas 157 mg; Sod 317 mg.

Sue Knotts, West Virginia

Frosty Pumpkin Delight

2 cups canned pumpkin

1/2 cup packed brown sugar

1/2 teaspoon cinnamon

1/4 teaspoon ginger

1/4 teaspoon nutmeg

1 quart vanilla ice cream, softened

Combine pumpkin, brown sugar and spices in bowl; mix well. Add ice cream; blend well. Spoon into loaf pan. Freeze until firm. Remove from pan; slice with warm knife.
Yield: 8 servings.

Approx Per Serving:
Cal 236; Prot 3 g; Carbo 31 g; T Fat 12 g; Chol 42 mg; Potas 265 mg; Sod 173 mg.

Merry Kramer, Oklahoma

RHUBARB DESSERT

4 cups chopped rhubarb
1 cup sugar
1 3-ounce package strawberry gelatin
1½ cups water
1 2-layer package white cake mix
1 stick butter, sliced

Place rhubarb in 9x13-inch baking dish. Sprinkle sugar and gelatin over rhubarb. Drizzle water over all. Sprinkle cake mix over top. Dot with butter. Bake at 350 degrees for 45 minutes or until golden brown.
Yield: 12 servings.

Approx Per Serving:
Cal 340; Prot 3 g; Carbo 58 g; T Fat 11 g; Chol 24 mg; Potas 43 mg; Sod 520 mg.

Jane Reed, Missouri

STRAWBERRY ICE CREAM SODA

2 3-ounce packages strawberry gelatin
2 cups hot water
1 cup cold water
1 24-ounce bottle of ginger ale, chilled
1 quart vanilla ice cream

Dissolve gelatin in hot water in bowl. Stir in cold water. Chill for 1 hour or until syrupy. Pour ½ cup mixture into each of 6 chilled 16-ounce glasses. Pour half the ginger ale gently into glasses. Spoon in ice cream. Fill with remaining ginger ale. Garnish with whole strawberries. Yield: 6 servings.

Approx Per Serving:
Cal 323; Prot 6 g; Carbo 56 g; T Fat 10 g; Chol 39 mg; Potas 173 mg; Sod 175 mg.

Virginia Hargrove, Georgia

STRAWBERRY REFRIGERATOR DESSERT

1 12-ounce angel food cake, torn
1 6-ounce package strawberry gelatin
2 cups boiling water
2 16-ounce packages frozen strawberries
1 6-ounce package vanilla instant pudding mix
2½ cups milk
8 ounces whipped topping

Place cake pieces in 9x13-inch pan. Dissolve gelatin in boiling water in bowl. Add strawberries; stir until strawberries thaw. Pour over cake. Chill until set. Prepare pudding mix with milk using package directions. Fold in whipped topping. Spread over congealed layer. Store in refrigerator. Yield: 15 servings.

Approx Per Serving:
Cal 422; Prot 14 g; Carbo 58 g; T Fat 16 g; Chol 49 mg; Potas 366 mg; Sod 1190 mg.

Emily Barton, Michigan

BANANA AND PINEAPPLE TWINKIE DESSERT

1   10-ounce package Twinkies

1   6-ounce package French vanilla instant pudding mix

3 cups milk

4 bananas, sliced

1   8-ounce can crushed pineapple, drained

8 ounces whipped topping

Cut Twinkies into small pieces. Place in 9x13-inch glass dish. Prepare pudding mix with milk using package directions. Layer bananas, pineapple, pudding and whipped topping over Twinkies. Chill until serving time. Yield: 12 servings.

Approx Per Serving:
Cal 324; Prot 4 g; Carbo 56 g; T Fat 11 g; Chol 8 mg; Potas 276 mg; Sod 283 mg.

Sandra Laughlin, Indiana

TWINKIE SURPRISE

1   10-ounce package Twinkies

2   4-ounce packages vanilla instant pudding mix

3 cups milk

8 ounces whipped topping

2   1-ounce Heath bars, chopped

Cut Twinkies into halves lengthwise. Arrange cream side up in 9x13-inch dish. Combine milk and pudding mix in bowl; beat until thick. Spread over Twinkies. Top with whipped topping and chopped candy. Chill for 1 hour or longer. Yield: 16 servings.

Approx Per Serving:
Cal 202; Prot 2 g; Carbo 28 g; T Fat 9 g; Chol 9 mg; Potas 86 mg; Sod 169 mg.

Dorothy L. Kalissa, California

RAISIN AND APPLE CAKE

1¹/₂ cups oil

2 cups sugar

3 eggs

1 teaspoon vanilla extract

2 cups all-purpose flour

1 cup whole wheat flour

1 teaspoon soda

1 teaspoon cinnamon

¹/₂ teaspoon salt

¹/₄ teaspoon nutmeg

2 cups chopped peeled apples

1 cup raisins

³/₄ cup finely chopped walnuts

Beat oil and sugar in mixer bowl until thick. Add eggs 1 at a time, beating well after each addition. Blend in vanilla. Sift in flour, whole wheat flour, soda, cinnamon, salt and nutmeg. Stir in apples, raisins and walnuts. Pour into greased and floured 10-inch cake pan. Bake at 325 degrees for 1 hour and 5 minutes. Cool in pan on wire rack for 15 minutes. Remove to cake plate to cool completely. Store, wrapped in foil, before slicing. Yield: 12 servings.

Photograph for this recipe is on page 69.

Sour Cream Banana Cake

1/4 cup margarine, softened
1 1/3 cups sugar
2 eggs
1 teaspoon vanilla extract
2 cups flour
1 teaspoon soda
3/4 teaspoon salt
1 cup sour cream
1 cup mashed bananas

Cream margarine and sugar in mixer bowl until light and fluffy. Beat in eggs and vanilla. Add sifted flour, soda and salt alternately with sour cream, mixing well after each addition. Stir in bananas. Pour into greased tube pan. Bake at 350 degrees for 40 to 45 minutes or until cake tests done. Remove to wire rack to cool. May add chopped pecans if desired.
Yield: 16 servings.

Approx Per Serving:
Cal 200; Prot 3 g; Carbo 32 g; T Fat 7 g;
Chol 41 mg; Potas 101 mg; Sod 202 mg.

Olga Roberts, Alabama

Butternut Cake

1 cup butter-flavor shortening
2 cups sugar
4 eggs
2 cups self-rising flour
1 cup milk
1 to 2 tablespoons butternut flavoring

Cream shortening and sugar in mixer bowl until light. Beat in eggs. Add flour alternately with milk, mixing well after each addition. Add butternut flavoring; mix well. Pour into 3 greased and floured 9-inch cake pans. Bake at 350 degrees for 30 minutes or until cake tests done. Remove to wire rack to cool. Frost with favorite frosting. Yield: 16 servings.

Approx Per Serving:
Cal 294; Prot 4 g; Carbo 37 g; T Fat 15 g;
Chol 55 mg; Potas 52 mg; Sod 193 mg.

Ellen Weyer, Colorado

Pantry Shelf Chocolate Cake

1   2-layer package German chocolate cake mix
1   14-ounce can sweetened condensed milk
1   12-ounce jar caramel ice cream topping
12 ounces whipped topping
3   1-ounce Heath bars, finely chopped

Prepare and bake cake mix using package directions for 9x13-inch cake. Punch holes in top of warm cake with end of wooden spoon. Pour sweetened condensed milk into holes. Pour ice cream topping into same holes. Spread with whipped topping. Sprinkle with candy. Store in refrigerator. Yield: 15 servings.

Approx Per Serving:
Cal 497; Prot 6 g; Carbo 68 g; T Fat 22 g;
Chol 64 mg; Potas 140 mg; Sod 349 mg.

Lea Ann Bishop, Iowa

EASY CARROT CAKE

1   2-layer package yellow cake mix

1¼ cups mayonnaise-type salad dressing

4 eggs

¼ cup cold water

2 teaspoons cinnamon

2 cups finely shredded carrots

½ cup chopped walnuts

1   16-ounce can vanilla frosting

Combine cake mix, salad dressing, eggs, water and cinnamon in mixer bowl; beat until well blended. Stir in carrots and walnuts. Pour into greased 9x13-inch cake pan. Bake at 350 degrees for 35 minutes or until cake tests done. Cool. Spread frosting over top. Yield: 12 servings.

Approx Per Serving:
Cal 500; Prot 5 g; Carbo 68 g; T Fat 17 g; Chol 77 mg; Potas 108 mg; Sod 547 mg.

Joanne Marlow, Iowa

EASY CHOCOLATE CAKE

1   4-ounce package chocolate pudding and pie filling mix

1   2-layer package chocolate cake mix

1 cup chocolate chips

Cook pudding using package directions. Combine with dry cake mix in bowl; mix well. Pour into greased and floured 9x13-inch cake pan. Sprinkle with chocolate chips. Bake at 350 degrees for 20 minutes. Yield: 12 servings.

Approx Per Serving:
Cal 386; Prot 21 g; Carbo 51 g; T Fat 19 g; Chol 5 mg; Potas 69 mg; Sod 329 mg.

Esther Molloy, Mississippi

CHOCOLATE CUPCAKES

4 ounces semisweet chocolate

1 cup margarine

1 teaspoon vanilla extract

2 cups chopped pecans

1 cup flour

1¾ cups sugar

4 eggs

Melt chocolate and margarine in saucepan. Stir in vanilla and pecans. Combine flour, sugar and eggs in mixer bowl; mix well. Add chocolate mixture; mix well. Spoon into paper-lined muffin cups. Bake at 350 degrees for 30 minutes. Remove to wire rack to cool. May bake in miniature muffin cups for 15 minutes if preferred. Yield: 24 servings.

Approx Per Serving:
Cal 246; Prot 3 g; Carbo 23 g; T Fat 17 g; Chol 46 mg; Potas 76 mg; Sod 102 mg.

Gaynell Richey, Kansas

Surpise Chocolate Cupcakes

1   2-layer package devil's food cake mix
3 eggs
1/2 cup oil
1 egg, beaten
8 ounces cream cheese, softened
1/2 cup sugar
1 cup semisweet chocolate chips

Prepare cake mix with 3 eggs, oil and water according to package directions. Fill paper-lined miniature muffin cups 2/3 full. Combine egg, cream cheese and sugar in bowl; mix well. Stir in chocolate chips. Place 1 teaspoonful chocolate chip mixture in each prepared muffin cup. Bake according to package directions. Yield: 24 servings.

Approx Per Serving:
Cal 229; Prot 3 g; Carbo 26 g; T Fat 13 g; Chol 46 mg; Potas 47 mg; Sod 172 mg.

Darlene Waymon, Texas

Devil's Food Pudding Cake

1   2-layer package devil's food cake mix
3 eggs
1/2 cup oil
1   4-ounce package vanilla instant pudding mix
1   4-ounce package chocolate instant pudding mix
4 cups milk
8 ounces whipped topping

Prepare cake mix with eggs, oil and water according to package directions. Pour into greased and floured 9x13-inch cake pan. Bake at 350 degrees for 40 minutes or until cake tests done. Cool. Prepare each pudding mix with 2 cups milk using package directions. Layer vanilla pudding and chocolate pudding over cake. Top with whipped topping. Chill until serving time. Yield: 15 servings.

Approx Per Serving:
Cal 248; Prot 2 g; Carbo 35 g; T Fat 11 g; Chol 32 mg; Potas 13 mg; Sod 246 mg.

Shirley Harper, West Virginia

Easy Chocolate Chip Cake

1   2-layer package butter cake mix
1   4-ounce package chocolate instant pudding mix
1/2 cup oil
1/2 cup water
4 eggs
1 cup sour cream
1 cup chocolate chips

Combine cake mix, pudding mix, oil, water, eggs and sour cream in mixer bowl. Beat for 2 minutes or until well blended. Stir in chocolate chips. Pour into greased and floured tube pan. Bake at 350 degrees for 1 hour or until cake tests done. Yield: 15 servings.

Approx Per Serving:
Cal 350; Prot 4 g; Carbo 43 g; T Fat 19 g; Chol 64 mg; Potas 79 mg; Sod 288 mg.

Maggie Francis, Kansas

MOIST AND CREAMY COCONUT CAKE

1   2-layer package yellow cake
       mix

1½ cups milk

½ cup sugar

2 cups flaked coconut

8 ounces whipped topping

Prepare and bake cake mix according to package directions for 9x13-inch cake pan. Cool for 15 minutes. Combine milk, sugar and ¼ cup coconut in saucepan. Bring to a boil; reduce heat. Simmer for 1 minute, stirring constantly. Punch holes in cake with fork. Pour milk mixture over cake. Cool completely. Fold ½ cup coconut into whipped topping. Spread over cake. Sprinkle remaining coconut over cake. Store in refrigerator. Yield: 12 servings.

Approx Per Serving:
Cal 471; Prot 5 g; Carbo 57 g; T Fat 25 g;
Chol 57 mg; Potas 113 mg; Sod 338 mg.

Sharon Marlow, Georgia

GINGER CAKE

½ cup shortening

1 cup sugar

1 cup molasses

2½ cups sifted flour

1¾ teaspoons soda

Ginger, cinnamon, cloves and
salt to taste

1 cup boiling water

2 eggs, beaten

Cream shortening, sugar and molasses in mixer bowl until light and fluffy. Sift flour, soda, spices and salt together. Add to creamed mixture alternately with water, mixing well after each addition. Mix in eggs. Pour into greased 9x13-inch cake pan. Bake at 350 degrees for 30 minutes or until cake tests done.
Yield: 12 servings.

Approx Per Serving:
Cal 297; Prot 4 g; Carbo 50 g; T Fat 10 g;
Chol 46 mg; Potas 815 mg; Sod 157 mg.

Amy M. Smith, West Virginia

LEMON BUNDT CAKE

1 small package lemon gelatin

1 cup boiling water

½ cup oil

1   2-layer package yellow
       cake mix

4 eggs

½ teaspoon lemon extract

Dissolve gelatin in water in bowl. Add oil and cake mix; mix well. Beat in eggs 1 at a time. Stir in lemon extract. Pour into greased and floured bundt pan. Bake at 350 degrees for 40 minutes. Invert onto wire rack to cool. Yield: 16 servings.

Approx Per Serving:
Cal 237; Prot 3 g; Carbo 32 g; T Fat 11 g;
Chol 69 mg; Potas 16 mg; Sod 231 mg.

Frances Carson, South Carolina

SPECIAL LEMON CAKE

1   2-layer package lemon cake mix
1/2 cup sugar
4 eggs
1/2 cup oil
1 cup apricot nectar
1 cup confectioners' sugar
2 tablespoons lemon juice

Combine cake mix, sugar, eggs, oil and apricot nectar in mixer bowl. Beat until well blended. Beat at medium speed for 2 minutes. Pour into greased and floured bundt pan. Bake at 350 degrees for 45 to 55 minutes or until cake tests done. Cool in pan for 25 minutes. Invert onto wire rack to cool. Drizzle with mixture of confectioners' sugar and lemon juice. Yield: 16 servings.

Approx Per Serving:
Cal 274; Prot 3 g; Carbo 42 g; T Fat 11 g; Chol 69 mg; Potas 37 mg; Sod 215 mg.

Gertrude Leaner, Maryland

PEANUT BUTTER AND JELLY CAKE

1   2-layer package butter-recipe golden cake mix
1 cup buttermilk
1/2 cup oil
1/4 cup honey
4 eggs
1/4 cup water
1/2 cup peanut butter
1 cup blackberry jelly

Combine cake mix, buttermilk, oil, honey, eggs and water in bowl. Beat at high speed for 2 minutes. Pour into 3 greased and floured 9-inch cake pans. Bake at 375 degrees for 25 minutes. Remove to wire rack to cool. Spread peanut butter and jelly between layers and over top of cake. Yield: 16 servings.

Approx Per Serving:
Cal 336; Prot 6 g; Carbo 46 g; T Fat 15 g; Chol 69 mg; Potas 113 mg; Sod 267 mg.

Tricia Wallach, Illinois

PISTACHIO CAKE

1   2-layer package white cake mix
1   4-ounce package pistachio instant pudding mix
3 eggs
1 cup club soda
1 cup oil
1   4-ounce package pistachio instant pudding mix
1 1/2 cups milk
8 ounces whipped topping

Combine cake mix and 1 package pudding mix in mixer bowl; mix well. Beat in eggs 1 at a time. Add club soda and oil; mix well. Spoon into greased and floured 9x13-inch cake pan. Bake at 350 degrees for 35 minutes or until cake tests done. Cool in pan. Combine remaining package pudding mix and milk in bowl; mix well. Fold in whipped topping. Spread on cake. Store in refrigerator. Yield: 12 servings.

Approx Per Serving:
Cal 494; Prot 5 g; Carbo 55 g; T Fat 29 g; Chol 73 mg; Potas 62 mg; Sod 396 mg.

Janet Reese, Texas

POPPY SEED CAKE

1 2-layer package yellow
   cake mix

1 4-ounce package French
vanilla instant pudding mix

1/4 cup poppy seed

1/2 cup oil

1 cup water

4 eggs

Combine cake mix, pudding mix, poppy seed, oil and water in mixer bowl; mix well. Beat in eggs 1 at a time. Pour into greased and floured tube pan. Bake at 350 degrees for 45 minutes. Cool in pan for 15 minutes. Remove to wire rack to cool completely. Yield: 16 servings.

Approx Per Serving:
Cal 237; Prot 3 g; Carbo 32 g; T Fat 11 g;
Chol 69 mg; Potas 17 mg; Sod 249 mg.

Cora Briggs, Missouri

WHIPPED CREAM POUND CAKE

1 cup butter, softened

3 cups sugar

6 eggs

3 cups cake flour

1 cup whipping cream

1 teaspoon vanilla extract

1 teaspoon lemon extract

Cream butter and sugar in mixer bowl until fluffy. Beat in eggs 1 at a time. Add cake flour alternately with cream, mixing well after each addition. Stir in flavorings. Pour into greased and floured 12-inch tube pan. Place in cold oven. Bake at 350 degrees for 1 hour and 20 minutes. Cool on wire rack. Yield: 16 servings.

Approx Per Serving:
Cal 401; Prot 4 g; Carbo 54 g; T Fat 19 g;
Chol 154 mg; Potas 60 mg; Sod 130 mg.

Kay Siehl, West Virginia

STRAWBERRY CAKE

1 2-layer package yellow
   cake mix

2 eggs

1 cup sour cream

1/4 cup water

1 small package strawberry
gelatin

1 cup confectioners' sugar

Combine first 4 ingredients in mixer bowl. Beat at medium speed for 3 minutes. Layer batter and gelatin 1/2 at a time in greased and floured bundt pan. Bake at 350 degrees for 45 minutes or until cake tests done. Cool in pan for 10 minutes. Invert onto cake plate. Sprinkle with confectioners' sugar. Yield: 16 servings.

Approx Per Serving:
Cal 221; Prot 3 g; Carbo 38 g; T Fat 6 g;
Chol 41 mg; Potas 29 mg; Sod 230 mg.

Sarah Toombs, Colorado

STRAWBERRY UPSIDE-DOWN CAKE

1 8-ounce package miniature
marshmallows

1 2-layer package white
cake mix

4 cups mashed strawberries

1 small package strawberry
gelatin

Sprinkle marshmallows into greased 9x13-inch cake pan. Prepare cake batter using package directions. Pour into prepared pan. Mix strawberries and gelatin in bowl. Spoon over batter. Bake at 350 degrees for 45 to 50 minutes or until cake tests done. Cut cooled cake into squares. Invert servings onto serving plates. Marshmallows rise to top of cake and strawberries sink to bottom when baked. Yield: 12 servings.

Approx Per Serving:
Cal 411; Prot 5 g; Carbo 78 g; T Fat 11 g;
Chol 0 mg; Potas 184 mg; Sod 249 mg.

Lacy Finegan, Indiana

WACKY CAKE

3 cups flour

2 cups sugar

6 tablespoons baking cocoa

1 teaspoon salt

2 teaspoons soda

2 teaspoons vanilla extract

2 teaspoons vinegar

1/2 cup melted margarine

2 cups water

Sift dry ingredients into 9x13-inch cake pan. Make 3 wells in mixture. Pour vanilla, vinegar and margarine into separate wells. Add water; mix well. Bake at 350 degrees until cake tests done. Yield: 16 servings.

Approx Per Serving:
Cal 238; Prot 3 g; Carbo 44 g; T Fat 6 g;
Chol 0 mg; Potas 50 mg; Sod 304 mg.

Leila Stuckey, West Virginia

YUM-YUM CAKE

2 cups sugar

1 20-ounce can crushed
pineapple

1 teaspoon soda

1 teaspoon vanilla extract

2 cups flour

1/2 cup chopped pecans

1 cup sour cream

1/2 cup melted butter

3/4 cup sugar

Combine 2 cups sugar, pineapple, soda, vanilla, flour and pecans in bowl in order listed, mixing well after each addition. Pour into ungreased 9x13-inch cake pan. Bake at 350 degrees for 30 minutes or until cake tests done. Mix sour cream, butter and 3/4 cup sugar in bowl. Pour over cake. May sprinkle with additional pecans if desired. Yield: 12 servings.

Approx Per Serving:
Cal 411; Prot 3 g; Carbo 72 g; T Fat 13 g;
Chol 25 mg; Potas 106 mg; Sod 140 mg.

Lynda L. Appelt, Texas

BUTTERSCOTCH BARS

1/2 cup butter

1 cup peanut butter

2 cups butterscotch chips

1 10-ounce package miniature marshmallows

1 cup coconut

Combine butter, peanut butter and butterscotch chips in saucepan. Heat until melted, stirring constantly. Cool to lukewarm. Fold in marshmallows. Sprinkle coconut over bottom of 9x13-inch dish. Spread peanut butter mixture over coconut. Let stand until firm. Cut into bars. Yield: 24 servings.

Approx Per Serving:
Cal 221; Prot 4 g; Carbo 21 g; T Fat 15 g;
Chol 12 mg; Potas 126 mg; Sod 124 mg.

Lila Pope, Louisiana

MICROWAVE CARAMEL AND PECAN CLUSTERS

1/4 cup margarine

8 ounces caramels

2 tablespoons milk

3 1/2 cups cornflakes

1/2 cup chopped pecans

1/2 cup coconut

Combine margarine and caramels in glass dish. Microwave on High for 3 to 4 minutes or until melted, stirring once. Add milk; mix well. Stir in cornflakes, pecans and coconut. Drop by spoonfuls onto waxed paper. Let stand until firm. Yield: 24 servings.

Approx Per Serving:
Cal 84; Prot 1 g; Carbo 12 g; T Fat 4 g;
Chol 0 mg; Potas 27 mg; Sod 97 mg.

Joan Lipsey, Kentucky

COCONUT JOYS

1/2 cup melted butter

2 cups confectioners' sugar

3 cups coconut

2 squares unsweetened chocolate, melted

Combine butter, confectioners' sugar and coconut in bowl; mix well. Shape into balls. Make indentation in center of each ball. Fill with chocolate. Chill until firm. Store in refrigerator. Yield: 36 servings.

Approx Per Serving:
Cal 82; Prot 0 g; Carbo 9 g; T Fat 6 g;
Chol 8 mg; Potas 36 mg; Sod 46 mg.

Betsy Tollman, Virginia

Microwave Two-Minute Fudge

1 pound confectioners' sugar

1/2 cup butter

1/3 cup baking cocoa

1/4 cup milk

1 teaspoon vanilla extract

Place confectioners' sugar, butter, cocoa and milk in glass dish; do not mix. Microwave on High for 2 minutes. Add vanilla. Beat for 2 minutes or until thickened. Pour into buttered 8x8-inch dish. Let stand until firm. Cut into squares. Yield: 36 servings.

Approx Per Serving:
Cal 74; Prot 0 g; Carbo 13 g; T Fat 3 g;
Chol 7 mg; Potas 13 mg; Sod 23 mg.

Lenora Page, North Carolina

Energy Snacks

1 cup confectioners' sugar

1 cup crunchy peanut butter

1 cup semisweet chocolate chips

1 cup raisins

1/2 cup dry milk powder

2/3 cup coconut

Combine confectioners' sugar, peanut butter, chocolate chips, raisins and dry milk powder in bowl; mix well. Shape into balls. Roll in coconut, coating well. Yield: 60 servings.

Approx Per Serving:
Cal 60; Prot 2 g; Carbo 7 g; T Fat 4 g;
Chol 0 mg; Potas 72 mg; Sod 23 mg.

Kathleen Salyers, Illinois

Peanut Clusters

1 cup semisweet chocolate chips

2 cups butterscotch chips

1 1/2 cups peanuts

Melt chocolate chips and butterscotch chips in double boiler over hot water. Add peanuts; mix well. Drop by spoonfuls onto waxed paper-lined tray. Chill for 30 minutes. Store in airtight container. May add coconut, raisins, crispy rice cereal or other favorite ingredients. May substitute peanut butter chips for butterscotch chips. Yield: 16 servings.

Approx Per Serving:
Cal 186; Prot 5 g; Carbo 15 g; T Fat 14 g;
Chol 0 mg; Potas 170 mg; Sod 5 mg.

Sally Kaufmann, Colorado

PEANUT BUTTER CANDY

1 small package vanilla pudding and pie filling mix

1 cup sugar

½ cup milk

2 tablespoons peanut butter

2 tablespoons margarine

Combine pudding mix, sugar and milk in saucepan. Bring to a boil, stirring constantly. Cook for 3 minutes, stirring constantly; remove from heat. Add peanut butter and margarine. Beat vigorously with wooden spoon until stiff. Spread in buttered dish. Let stand until firm. Cut into squares. Yield: 16 servings.

Approx Per Serving:
Cal 97; Prot 1 g; Carbo 18 g; T Fat 3 g;
Chol 1 mg; Potas 26 mg; Sod 64 mg.

Alexandria Smith, Tennessee

SALTED PEANUT BARS

1   7-ounce jar marshmallow creme

2 cups peanut butter chips

1   14-ounce can sweetened condensed milk

1½ pounds salted peanuts

Combine marshmallow creme, peanut butter chips and condensed milk in saucepan. Heat until blended, stirring constantly. Layer half the peanuts, all the marshmallow mixture and remaining peanuts in 9x13-inch dish. Chill until firm. Cut into 1x1½-inch bars.
Yield: 78 servings.

Approx Per Serving:
Cal 104; Prot 3 g; Carbo 10 g; T Fat 7 g;
Chol 3 mg; Potas 96 mg; Sod 46 mg.

Michelle Miller, Florida

BANANA CONFETTI BARS

¾ cup butter, softened

1¼ cups packed brown sugar

1 egg

1 large banana, mashed

½ teaspoon lemon juice

1½ cups flour

½ teaspoon soda

¼ teaspoon salt

2 cups quick-cooking oats

1 cup "M&M's" Plain Chocolate Candies

Cream butter and brown sugar in mixer bowl until light and fluffy. Beat in egg, banana and lemon juice. Add mixture of flour, soda and salt; mix well. Stir in oats and ½ cup candies. Spread in greased 10x15-inch baking pan. Sprinkle with remaining candies. Bake at 350 degrees for 25 to 30 minutes or until golden brown. Cool on wire rack. Cut into bars. Yield: 35 servings.

Photograph for this recipe is on page 35.

BLONDE BROWNIES

2 cups packed light brown
sugar

²/₃ cup oil

2 eggs, slightly beaten

2 teaspoons vanilla extract

2 cups flour

1 teaspoon baking powder

¹/₄ teaspoon soda

1 teaspoon salt

Blend brown sugar and oil in bowl. Stir in eggs and vanilla. Add mixture of dry ingredients gradually, mixing well after each addition. Spoon into greased 9x13-inch baking pan. Bake at 350 degrees for 25 minutes; do not overbake. Cool in pan; cut into squares. May sprinkle with chocolate chips and pecans before baking if desired. Yield: 24 servings.

Approx Per Serving:
Cal 166; Prot 2 g; Carbo 26 g; T Fat 7 g;
Chol 23 mg; Potas 79 mg; Sod 124 mg.

Peggy Spieckermann, Missouri

EASY BROWNIES

4 ounces semisweet chocolate

1 cup margarine

¹/₂ teaspoon butter flavoring

1¹/₂ cups chopped pecans

1³/₄ cups sugar

1 cup flour

4 eggs

1 teaspoon vanilla extract

Melt chocolate and margarine in saucepan; mix well. Stir in butter flavoring and pecans. Combine sugar, flour, eggs and vanilla in bowl; mix just until moistened. Mix in chocolate mixture; do not beat. Pour into greased 9x13-inch baking pan. Bake at 350 degrees for 40 minutes. Yield: 15 servings.

Approx Per Serving:
Cal 368; Prot 4 g; Carbo 36 g; T Fat 25 g;
Chol 73 mg; Potas 105 mg; Sod 163 mg.

Charlotte Wolfe, West Virginia

FUDGE BROWNIES

¹/₂ cup butter, softened

1 cup sugar

1 teaspoon vanilla extract

2 eggs

2 ounces unsweetened
chocolate, melted

¹/₂ cup sifted flour

¹/₂ cup chopped walnuts

Cream butter, sugar and vanilla in mixer bowl until fluffy. Beat in eggs. Blend in chocolate. Stir in flour and walnuts. Spread in greased 8x8-inch baking pan. Bake at 325 degrees for 30 minutes. Cut into squares. Yield: 16 servings.

Approx Per Serving:
Cal 165; Prot 2 g; Carbo 17 g; T Fat 11 g;
Chol 50 mg; Potas 62 mg; Sod 58 mg.

Laurie Moore, California

GRANDMA'S BROWNIES

1/4 cup butter, softened

1 cup sugar

4 eggs

1 cup flour

1   16-ounce can chocolate syrup

3/4 cup chopped pecans

Cream butter and sugar in mixer bowl until fluffy. Beat in eggs 1 at a time. Stir in flour, chocolate syrup and pecans. Spoon into greased and floured 9x13-inch baking pan. Bake at 350 degrees for 30 minutes.
Yield: 24 servings.

Approx Per Serving:
Cal 149 ; Prot 2 g; Carbo 24 g; T Fat 6 g;
Chol 51 mg; Potas 74 mg; Sod 44 mg.

Kristi Litman, California

CHESS SQUARES

1   2-layer package
butter-recipe yellow cake mix

1 egg

1/2 cup butter, softened

1 pound confectioners' sugar

8 ounces cream cheese, softened

3 eggs

1 teaspoon vanilla extract

Combine cake mix, 1 egg and butter in bowl; mix with a fork. Pat into 9x13-inch baking pan. Combine confectioners' sugar, cream cheese, 3 eggs and vanilla in mixer bowl; mix well. Mixture will be lumpy. Pour over cake mix layer. Bake at 300 degrees for 45 minutes or until golden brown; do not overbake. Cool to room temperature. Cut into squares. Store in refrigerator. Yield: 24 servings.

Approx Per Serving:
Cal 210; Prot 10 g; Carbo 28 g; T Fat 10 g;
Chol 66 mg; Potas 19 mg; Sod 119 mg.

Karen Cronin, Kentucky

CHEWY BARS

1 cup melted butter

2 eggs

1 pound light brown sugar

2 cups flour

1 teaspoon baking powder

2 teaspoons vanilla extract

1/2 cup chopped pecans

Combine butter, eggs, brown sugar, flour, baking powder and vanilla in bowl; mix well. Stir in pecans. Spoon into greased 9x13-inch baking pan. Bake at 350 degrees for 20 to 30 minutes or until golden brown. Cool. Cut into bars. Yield: 36 servings.

Approx Per Serving:
Cal 133; Prot 1 g; Carbo 18 g; T Fat 7 g;
Chol 29 mg; Potas 62 mg; Sod 62 mg.

Margaret Doherty, Texas

CHOCOLATE CHERRY BARS

1 2-layer package devil's food
cake mix

1 21-ounce can cherry pie
filling

2 eggs, beaten

1 teaspoon almond extract

1 cup sugar

5 tablespoons margarine

1/3 cup milk

1 cup semisweet chocolate
chips

Combine cake mix, pie filling, eggs and almond extract in large bowl; mix well with wooden spoon. Spoon into greased and floured 10x15-inch baking pan. Bake at 350 degrees for 20 to 30 minutes or until layer tests done. Combine sugar, margarine and milk in saucepan. Bring to a boil, stirring constantly; remove from heat. Stir in chocolate chips. Pour over warm baked layer. Cool. Cut into bars. Yield: 36 servings.

Approx Per Serving:
Cal 160; Prot 2 g; Carbo 26 g; T Fat 6 g;
Chol 12 mg; Potas 42 mg; Sod 150 mg.

Goldie Wilson, Pennsylvania

CHOCOLATE COCONUT BARS

2 cups graham cracker crumbs

1/2 cup melted butter

1 14-ounce can sweetened
condensed milk

3 1/2 cups flaked coconut

10 ounces milk chocolate,
melted

Mix crumbs and butter in bowl. Pat into 9x13-inch baking pan. Bake at 350 degrees for 8 minutes. Mix condensed milk and coconut in bowl. Spread over baked layer. Bake at 350 degrees for 15 minutes or until brown. Drizzle with chocolate. Cool. Cut into bars. Yield: 24 servings.

Approx Per Serving:
Cal 412; Prot 37 g; Carbo 18 g; T Fat 21 g;
Chol 119 mg; Potas 399 mg; Sod 203 mg.

Livie Freeman, Arizona

DATE AND PECAN BARS

1 pound dates, cut into quarters

4 cups pecan halves

1 cup flour

1 teaspoon baking powder

1/4 teaspoon salt

3 eggs, beaten

1 cup sugar

1 teaspoon vanilla extract

Toss dates and pecans with a small amount of flour. Mix remaining flour with baking powder and salt in bowl. Combine eggs, sugar and vanilla in large bowl; mix well. Add dry ingredients; mix well. Fold in dates and pecans. Spoon into 2 greased and floured 9x13-inch baking pans. Bake at 300 degrees for 30 minutes or until brown. Cool completely. Cut into bars. Yield: 48 servings.

Approx Per Serving:
Cal 123; Prot 2 g; Carbo 15 g; T Fat 7 g;
Chol 17 mg; Potas 107 mg; Sod 23 mg.

Edith O. Wright, Florida

HELLO DOLLY BARS

1/2 cup butter
1 cup graham cracker crumbs
1 cup semisweet chocolate chips
1 cup coconut
1 cup chopped pecans
1 14-ounce can sweetened condensed milk

Melt butter in 9x13-inch baking dish. Layer cracker crumbs, chocolate chips, coconut and pecans in prepared dish. Drizzle sweetened condensed milk over layers; do not stir. Bake at 350 degrees for 30 minutes or until light brown. Cool completely. Cut into bars. Yield: 24 servings.

Approx Per Serving:
Cal 192; Prot 3 g; Carbo 19 g; T Fat 13 g;
Chol 16 mg; Potas 129 mg; Sod 93 mg.

Julie Geis, Oklahoma

LEMON BARS

1 cup shortening
1/4 teaspoon salt
1/2 cup confectioners' sugar
2 1/4 cups flour
4 eggs, beaten
2 cups sugar
5 tablespoons lemon juice

Combine shortening, salt, confectioners' sugar and 2 cups flour in bowl; mix well. Press into 9x13-inch baking dish. Bake at 350 degrees for 20 minutes. Combine remaining 1/4 cup flour with eggs, sugar and lemon juice in bowl; mix well. Pour over baked layer. Bake for 20 minutes longer. Garnish with additional confectioners' sugar if desired. Cool; cut into squares. Yield: 24 servings.

Approx Per Serving:
Cal 204; Prot 2 g; Carbo 28 g; T Fat 10 g;
Chol 46 mg; Potas 27 mg; Sod 34 mg.

Tammy Huckaby, Texas

LEMON CHEESE BARS

1 egg
1/3 cup oil
1 2-layer package pudding-recipe yellow cake mix
8 ounces cream cheese, softened
1/3 cup sugar
2 teaspoons lemon juice
1 egg

Combine 1 egg, oil and cake mix in bowl; mix well. Reserve 1 cup mixture. Press remaining mixture into 9x13-inch baking pan. Bake at 350 degrees for 15 minutes. Beat cream cheese, sugar, lemon juice and 1 egg in bowl until smooth. Spread over baked layer. Sprinkle with reserved cake mixture. Bake for 15 minutes longer. Cool completely. Cut into bars. Yield: 24 servings.

Approx Per Serving:
Cal 168; Prot 2 g; Carbo 21 g; T Fat 8 g;
Chol 33 mg; Potas 17 mg; Sod 165 mg.

Betsy Childress, Pennsylvania

FAST AND FANCY MACAROONS

1   14-ounce package coconut

1   14-ounce can sweetened
    condensed milk

2 teaspoons vanilla extract

1 cup miniature chocolate chips

60 maraschino cherry halves

Combine coconut, condensed milk, vanilla and chocolate chips in bowl; mix well. Drop by teaspoonfuls 1 inch apart onto well-greased cookie sheet. Place cherry half on each. Bake at 350 degrees for 10 to 12 minutes or until light brown. Remove from cookie sheet immediately with wet spatula. Cool on waxed paper-lined surface. Yield: 60 servings.

Approx Per Serving:
Cal 60; Prot 1 g; Carbo 6 g; T Fat 4 g;
Chol 2 mg; Potas 56 mg; Sod 25 mg.

Petra Longworth, New Mexico

OATMEAL COOKIE BARS

1   2¹/2-cup package oatmeal
    cookie mix

2 eggs

¹/2 cup oil

¹/3 cup chopped pecans

¹/3 cup raisins

Combine cookie mix, eggs and oil in bowl; mix well. Stir in pecans and raisins. Spread in greased 7x11-inch baking pan. Bake for 20 to 25 minutes or until brown. May substitute ¹/3 cup sunflower seed, coconut or chocolate chips for pecans and/or raisins. Yield: 24 servings.

Approx Per Serving:
Cal 166; Prot 2 g; Carbo 16 g; T Fat 11 g;
Chol 23 mg; Potas 82 mg; Sod 54 mg.

Mary McFie, California

NO-BAKE OATMEAL COOKIES

2 cups sugar

3 tablespoons (heaping) baking
cocoa

¹/2 cup margarine, softened

¹/2 cup milk

3 cups oats

¹/2 cup peanut butter

Mix sugar, cocoa, margarine and milk in saucepan. Bring to a boil. Cook for 3 minutes; remove from heat. Stir in oats and peanut butter. Drop by teaspoonfuls onto waxed paper. Let stand until firm. Yield: 30 servings.

Approx Per Serving:
Cal 139; Prot 3 g; Carbo 20 g; T Fat 6 g;
Chol 1 mg; Potas 72 mg; Sod 55 mg.

Carol Freeman, Tennessee

ORANGE BALLS

1   16-ounce package vanilla
    wafers, crushed

1/2 cup butter, softened

1 pound confectioners' sugar

1   6-ounce can frozen orange
    juice concentrate, thawed

1 cup chopped pecans

1 cup coconut

Combine cookie crumbs, butter, confectioners' sugar, orange juice concentrate and pecans in bowl; mix well. Shape into small balls. Roll in coconut. Store in refrigerator.
Yield: 72 servings.

Approx Per Serving:
Cal 84; Prot 1 g; Carbo 13 g; T Fat 4 g;
Chol 7 mg; Potas 34 mg; Sod 37 mg.

Melissa Thompson, Oklahoma

PEANUT BUTTER CUP BARS

1 cup melted margarine

2 1/2 cups graham cracker
crumbs

2 1/2 cups confectioners' sugar

1 cup peanut butter

2 cups chocolate chips, melted

Combine margarine, graham cracker crumbs, confectioners' sugar and peanut butter in bowl; mix well. Spread in buttered 9x13-inch pan. Spread melted chocolate evenly over top. Chill until firm. Cut into bars. Yield: 24 servings.

Approx Per Serving:
Cal 297; Prot 5 g; Carbo 30 g; T Fat 20 g;
Chol 0 mg; Potas 160 mg; Sod 212 mg.

Marilyn Gross, Illinois

PEANUT BUTTER AND JELLY BARS

3 cups flour

1 cup sugar

1 1/2 teaspoons baking powder

1/2 cup butter, softened

1/2 cup peanut butter

2 eggs, slightly beaten

1 cup grape jelly

Combine flour, sugar and baking powder in bowl. Cut in butter and peanut butter until crumbly. Add eggs; mix well. Press half the mixture into 9x13-inch baking pan. Spread with jelly. Crumble remaining dough over jelly. Bake at 375 degrees for 30 to 35 minutes or until light brown. Cool completely. Cut into bars.
Yield: 24 servings.

Approx Per Serving:
Cal 194; Prot 4 g; Carbo 30 g; T Fat 7 g;
Chol 33 mg; Potas 70 mg; Sod 83 mg.

Irene Reppard, West Virginia

Peanut Butter-Granola Bars

1/2 cup honey

2/3 cup peanut butter

3 cups granola

Bring honey to a boil in saucepan. Cook for 1 minute; remove from heat. Stir in peanut butter and granola. Press into buttered 9x9-inch pan. Cool completely. Cut into bars.
Yield: 15 servings.

Approx Per Serving:
Cal 202; Prot 6 g; Carbo 26 g; T Fat 10 g; Chol 0 mg; Potas 161 mg; Sod 93 mg.

Heather Wilette, Ohio

Easiest Peanut Butter Cookies

1 cup peanut butter

1 cup sugar

1 egg

Combine peanut butter and sugar in bowl; mix well. Mix in egg. Drop by small spoonfuls onto ungreased cookie sheet. Press lightly with fork in crisscross design. Bake at 375 degrees until light brown. Yield: 36 servings.

Approx Per Serving:
Cal 66; Prot 2 g; Carbo 7 g; T Fat 4 g; Chol 8 mg; Potas 51 mg; Sod 31 mg.

Susan Woodall, Tennessee

Pull Apart S'Mores

Peanut butter

24 graham cracker squares

4 cups miniature marshmallows

1 1/3 cups "M&M's" Plain Chocolate Candies

Spread peanut butter lightly on graham crackers. Arrange crackers in single layer in 10x15-inch baking pan. Sprinkle with marshmallows and candies. Broil 6 inches from heat source in preheated broiler for 2 minutes or until light brown. Press candies lightly into melted marshmallows. Serve immediately.
Yield: 2 dozen.

Photograph for this recipe is on page 35.

APPLE CHESS PIE

1/2 cup melted margarine

1 1/2 cups sugar

1 1/2 teaspoons vinegar

1 1/2 teaspoons cornmeal

3 eggs, slightly beaten

1 1/2 cups applesauce

1 unbaked deep-dish 9-inch pie shell

Combine margarine, sugar, vinegar and cornmeal in bowl; mix well. Add eggs; stir until just mixed. Spread applesauce in pie shell. Pour cornmeal mixture over applesauce. Bake at 425 degrees for 10 minutes. Reduce temperature to 275 degrees. Bake for 40 minutes or until set. Yield: 8 servings.

Approx Per Serving:
Cal 410; Prot 4 g; Carbo 53 g; T Fat 21 g; Chol 80 mg; Potas 79 mg; Sod 299 mg.

Pam Crider, Mississippi

APPLESAUCE PIE

2 cups flour

2 teaspoons salt

2/3 cup shortening

5 to 7 tablespoons cold water

2   16-ounce cans applesauce

1/2 cup sugar

3 tablespoons flour

1 teaspoon cinnamon

Mix 2 cups flour and salt in bowl. Cut in shortening until crumbly. Sprinkle with enough cold water to form soft dough. Roll into two 1/8-inch thick circles. Place 1 circle in pie plate. Mix applesauce, sugar, 3 tablespoons flour and cinnamon in bowl. Spoon into prepared pie plate; top with remaining pastry. Seal edges; cut vents. Bake at 425 degrees for 20 minutes. Reduce temperature to 375 degrees. Bake for 40 minutes longer. Yield: 8 servings.

Approx Per Serving:
Cal 409; Prot 4 g; Carbo 61 g; T Fat 18 g; Chol 0 mg; Potas 102 mg; Sod 538 mg.

Mary V. Coffman, West Virginia

BUTTERMILK PIE

1/2 cup buttermilk

1/2 cup melted butter

1 tablespoon flour

1 teaspoon vanilla extract

4 eggs

1 1/2 cups sugar

1 unbaked 9-inch pie shell

Combine buttermilk, butter, flour, vanilla, eggs and sugar in bowl; mix well. Pour into pie shell. Bake at 350 degrees for 45 minutes. Yield: 6 servings.

Approx Per Serving:
Cal 544; Prot 7 g; Carbo 65 g; T Fat 29 g; Chol 225 mg; Potas 97 mg; Sod 381 mg.

Myra Roberts, Tennessee

CARAMEL PIES

1   7-ounce can coconut

1   4-ounce package sliced
    almonds

¼ cup melted butter

8 ounces cream cheese, softened

1½ cups confectioner's sugar

8 ounces whipped topping

2   graham cracker pie shells

1   10-ounce jar caramel ice
    cream topping

Combine coconut, almonds and butter in bowl; mix well. Spread on baking sheet. Broil until golden brown. Cool. Beat cream cheese and confectioners' sugar in mixer bowl until light and fluffy. Fold in whipped topping. Spoon into pie shells. Sprinkle with coconut mixture; drizzle caramel topping over top. Chill until serving time. Yield: 16 servings.

Approx Per Serving:
Cal 527; Prot 5 g; Carbo 62 g; T Fat 30 g;
Chol 23 mg; Potas 189 mg; Sod 396 mg.

Winnie Judge, California

CHERRY CHEESE PIE

8 ounces cream cheese, softened

1   14-ounce can sweetened
    condensed milk

⅓ cup lemon juice

1 teaspoon vanilla extract

1 graham cracker pie shell

1   21-ounce can cherry pie
    filling, chilled

Beat cream cheese in bowl until fluffy. Blend in sweetened condensed milk. Stir in lemon juice and vanilla. Pour into pie shell. Chill for 3 hours or until firm. Top with pie filling. Chill until serving time. Yield: 6 servings.

Approx Per Serving:
Cal 714; Prot 11 g; Carbo 97 g; T Fat 34 g;
Chol 64 mg; Potas 470 mg; Sod 544 mg.

Jessica Walters, Arkansas

CREAMY ICEBOX CHERRY PIE

1   3-ounce package cherry
    gelatin

1 cup boiling water

1 pint vanilla ice cream

1   16-ounce can Bing cherries,
    drained

1 baked pie shell

Dissolve gelatin in boiling water in bowl. Chill until partially set. Beat ice cream in mixer bowl until soft. Add gelatin; beat well. Fold in cherries. Spoon into pie shell. Chill until serving time. Yield: 6 servings.

Approx Per Serving:
Cal 381; Prot 6 g; Carbo 58 g; T Fat 15 g;
Chol 20 mg; Potas 298 mg; Sod 268 mg.

Barbara Dotson, New York

IMPOSSIBLE CHERRY STREUSEL PIE

1 cup milk

2 tablespoons margarine, softened

2 eggs

1/4 teaspoon almond extract

1/2 cup buttermilk baking mix

1/4 cup sugar

1 21-ounce can cherry pie filling

1/4 cup buttermilk baking mix

2 tablespoons margarine, softened

1/2 cup packed brown sugar

1/2 teaspoon cinnamon

Combine milk, 2 tablespoons margarine, eggs, almond extract, 1/2 cup baking mix and sugar in bowl. Beat until well mixed. Pour into greased 10-inch pie plate. Spoon pie filling over batter. Bake at 400 degrees for 25 minutes. Sprinkle mixture of 1/4 cup baking mix, 2 tablespoons margarine, brown sugar and cinnamon over top. Bake for 10 minutes longer.
Yield: 8 servings.

Approx Per Serving:
Cal 367; Prot 5 g; Carbo 56 g; T Fat 14 g; Chol 57 mg; Potas 205 mg; Sod 424 mg.

Eliza Delayne, Oklahoma

UPSIDE-DOWN CHERRY PIE

1 21-ounce can cherry pie filling

1 tablespoon butter

3/4 cup flour

1/2 cup sugar

2 teaspoons baking powder

1/2 cup milk

Pour pie filling into 10-inch deep-dish pie plate spread with 1 tablespoon butter. Combine flour, sugar and baking powder in bowl; mix well. Stir in milk. Pour batter over pie filling. Bake at 350 degrees for 20 minutes or until crust is brown.
Yield: 8 servings.

Approx Per Serving:
Cal 265; Prot 3 g; Carbo 50 g; T Fat 7 g; Chol 6 mg; Potas 114 mg; Sod 273 mg.

Arlene Simpson, South Carolina

SOUR CREAM CHERRY PIE

1 16-ounce can sour cherries

1 unbaked 8-inch pie shell

1 cup sugar

1/2 teaspoon vanilla extract

2 cups sour cream

3 tablespoons flour

Drain cherries, reserving 3 tablespoons juice. Place cherries in pie shell. Sprinkle with 1 tablespoon sugar. Combine remaining sugar, reserved juice, vanilla, sour cream and flour in bowl; mix well. Pour over cherries. Bake at 325 degrees for 1 hour or until brown. Yield: 8 servings.

Approx Per Serving:
Cal 364; Prot 4 g; Carbo 45 g; T Fat 20 g; Chol 26 mg; Potas 153 mg; Sod 173 mg.

Donna Borstad, California

CHOCOLATE-ALMOND PIE

6   1-ounce chocolate-almond
     candy bars

16 large marshmallows

½ cup milk

1 cup whipping cream,
     whipped

1   9-inch graham cracker pie
     shell

Melt candy bars and marshmallows in milk in top of double boiler; mix well. Cool to room temperature. Fold in whipped cream. Spoon into pie shell. Chill until serving time.
Yield: 8 servings.

Approx Per Serving:
Cal 331; Prot 4 g; Carbo 36 g; T Fat 19 g;
Chol 22 mg; Potas 44 mg; Sod 162 mg.

Mandy Van Hoozer, Texas

COOL AND CREAMY CHOCOLATE PIE

3 ounces cream cheese, softened

¼ cup sugar

1 teaspoon vanilla extract

½ cup chocolate syrup

1 cup whipping cream, chilled

1   8-inch crumb pie shell

Combine cream cheese, sugar and vanilla in mixer bowl; beat until smooth. Beat in chocolate syrup until blended. Beat whipping cream in chilled mixer bowl until soft peaks form. Fold gently into chocolate mixture. Pour into pie shell. Freeze, covered, until firm. Garnish with fresh fruit and chocolate curls.
Yield: 8 servings.

Photograph for this recipe is on page 17.

CLOUD PIES

5 tablespoons lemon juice

1   14-ounce can sweetened
     condensed milk

1   16-ounce can crushed
     pineapple, drained

8 ounces whipped topping

1¼ cups chopped pecans

2   8-inch graham cracker pie
     shells

Combine lemon juice and condensed milk in bowl; mix well. Add pineapple, whipped topping and pecans; mix well. Spoon into pie shells. Chill until serving time.
Yield: 16 servings.

Approx Per Serving:
Cal 407; Prot 5 g; Carbo 48 g; T Fat 23 g;
Chol 8 mg; Potas 230 mg; Sod 274 mg.

Billie Fitts, Texas

COCONUT CUSTARD PIE

6 egg yolks
1 cup sugar
2¹/₂ cups milk
¹/₂ cup coconut
6 egg whites
1 unbaked 9-inch pie shell

Beat egg yolks in mixer bowl. Add sugar 1 tablespoon at a time, beating constantly. Add milk; mix well. Stir in coconut. Beat egg whites in small bowl for 1 minute. Fold gently into coconut mixture. Spoon into pie shell. Bake at 350 degrees for 1 hour. Yield: 6 servings.

Approx Per Serving:
Cal 449; Prot 12 g; Carbo 55 g; T Fat 21 g;
Chol 288 mg; Potas 237 mg; Sod 311 mg.

Arlene Heck, Pennsylvania

THREE-MINUTE FRENCH COCONUT PIE

¹/₄ cup melted margarine
1 cup sugar
3 eggs
¹/₄ cup buttermilk
1 teaspoon vanilla extract
1 cup coconut
1 unbaked 8-inch pie shell

Combine margarine, sugar, eggs, buttermilk and vanilla in bowl; mix well. Stir in coconut. Pour into pie shell. Bake at 325 degrees for 35 to 45 minutes or until set. Yield: 8 servings.

Approx Per Serving:
Cal 352; Prot 4 g; Carbo 41 g; T Fat 20 g;
Chol 80 mg; Potas 90 mg; Sod 269 mg.

Velma McCardell, Wisconsin

CRANBERRY PIE

2 cups cranberries
¹/₂ cup chopped pecans
¹/₂ cup sugar
¹/₄ cup melted butter
2 eggs, beaten
1 cup sugar
1 cup sifted flour
¹/₂ cup melted butter

Place cranberries in greased pie plate. Sprinkle with pecans and ¹/₂ cup sugar. Drizzle with ¹/₄ cup butter. Combine remaining ingredients in bowl; mix well. Pour over cranberries; do not mix. Bake at 325 degrees for 40 to 50 minutes or until golden brown. Serve warm with ice cream or whipped cream. Yield: 8 servings.

Approx Per Serving:
Cal 430; Prot 4 g; Carbo 53 g; T Fat 24 g;
Chol 115 mg; Potas 83 mg; Sod 164 mg.

Barbara Boyden, Rhode Island

CREAM CHEESE PIE

12 ounces cream cheese, softened

1/2 cup sugar

2 eggs

1/2 teaspoon vanilla extract

1 9-inch graham cracker pie shell

3/4 cup sour cream

2 tablespoons sugar

1/2 teaspoon vanilla extract

Beat cream cheese in bowl until smooth. Add 1/2 cup sugar, eggs and 1/2 teaspoon vanilla; mix well. Spoon into pie shell. Bake at 350 degrees for 20 minutes. Blend sour cream, 2 tablespoons sugar and 1/2 teaspoon vanilla in bowl. Spread over pie. Bake for 5 to 10 minutes longer or until set. Chill until serving time. Yield: 6 servings.

Approx Per Serving:
Cal 638; Prot 10 g; Carbo 58 g; T Fat 42 g; Chol 166 mg; Potas 215 mg; Sod 525 mg.

Ruth P. Rice, Maryland

GRASSHOPPER PIE

24 Oreo cookies, finely crushed

1/4 cup melted butter

1/4 cup milk

1 teaspoon peppermint extract

1 13-ounce jar marshmallow creme

2 cups whipping cream, whipped

Combine cookie crumbs and butter in bowl; mix well. Reserve 1/2 cup mixture. Press remaining crumbs into 10-inch deep-dish pie plate. Blend milk, peppermint extract and marshmallow creme in bowl. Add green food coloring if desired. Fold in whipped cream gently. Pour into prepared pie plate; sprinkle with reserved crumbs. Freeze overnight. Yield: 8 servings.

Approx Per Serving:
Cal 553; Prot 3 g; Carbo 61 g; T Fat 34 g; Chol 98 mg; Potas 121 mg; Sod 242 mg.

Cris Harper, Texas

ICE CREAM PIE

1/2 gallon favorite ice cream, softened

1 9-inch chocolate crumb pie shell

4 or 5 Oreo cookies, crushed

Spoon ice cream into pie shell. Top with crumbs. Store in freezer. Yield: 8 servings.

Approx Per Serving:
Cal 504; Prot 7 g; Carbo 62 g; T Fat 26 g; Chol 59 mg; Potas 330 mg; Sod 384 mg.

Tracy Markham, Indiana

QUICK KEY LIME PIE

20 butter crackers

1 14-ounce can sweetened
    condensed milk

¼ cup Key lime juice

8 ounces whipped topping

Line 9-inch pie plate with whole crackers. Combine sweetened condensed milk and lime juice in bowl; mix well. Fold in whipped topping. Spoon into prepared pie plate. Freeze until firm. Yield: 6 servings.

Approx Per Serving:
Cal 385; Prot 6 g; Carbo 52 g; T Fat 19 g;
Chol 23 mg; Potas 274 mg; Sod 195 mg.

Dolores Sandusky, Arizona

PEANUT BUTTER PIE

½ cup peanut butter

1 cup confectioners' sugar

3 ounces cream cheese, softened

8 ounces whipped topping

1 baked 9-inch pie shell

Blend peanut butter, confectioners' sugar and cream cheese in mixer bowl until creamy. Fold in whipped topping. Spoon into pie shell. Chill until serving time. Yield: 6 servings.

Approx Per Serving:
Cal 511; Prot 9 g; Carbo 42 g; T Fat 36 g;
Chol 16 mg; Potas 187 mg; Sod 322 mg.

Joyce Ann Kisner, Maryland

PUMPKIN PIE

½ cup packed brown sugar

8 ounces cream cheese, softened

2 eggs

⅔ cup canned pumpkin

¾ teaspoon pumpkin pie spice

1 8-inch graham cracker
    pie shell

Cream brown sugar and cream cheese in mixer bowl until fluffy. Beat in eggs. Add pumpkin and spice; mix well. Spoon into pie shell. Bake at 350 degrees for 35 minutes. Cool to room temperature. Chill until serving time. Yield: 6 servings.

Approx Per Serving:
Cal 508; Prot 7 g; Carbo 55 g; T Fat 30 g;
Chol 133 mg; Potas 269 mg; Sod 463 mg.

Dorothy Irwin, Louisiana

Frozen Strawberry Pie

8 ounces cream cheese, softened

1/2 cup sugar

1 cup sour cream

2 10-ounce packages frozen strawberries, thawed, drained

1 8-inch graham cracker pie shell

Beat cream cheese and sugar in mixer bowl until fluffy. Fold in sour cream and strawberries. Spoon into pie shell. Freeze for 8 hours to overnight. Let stand at room temperature for 30 minutes before serving. Yield: 6 servings.

Approx Per Serving:
Cal 642; Prot 7 g; Carbo 78 g; T Fat 36 g; Chol 58 mg; Potas 277 mg; Sod 454 mg.

Darlene M. Fleck, California

Fruit Tart

1 cup flour

1 tablespoon sugar

1 tablespoon butter

8 ounces cream cheese, softened

1 cup confectioners' sugar

16 ounces whipped topping

1 21-ounce can peach pie filling

Mix flour, sugar and butter in bowl. Press into circle on baking sheet. Bake at 350 degrees for 20 minutes or until golden brown. Cool. Beat cream cheese and confectioners' sugar in bowl until fluffy. Fold in whipped topping. Spread on baked layer. Spoon pie filling over top. Chill until serving time. Yield: 8 servings.

Approx Per Serving:
Cal 564; Prot 5 g; Carbo 82 g; T Fat 26 g; Chol 35 mg; Potas 120 mg; Sod 134 mg.

George Ann Jackson, Florida

Praline Tarts

1/4 cup margarine

1/3 cup packed brown sugar

1 1/2 cups chopped pecans

12 baked tart shells

2 cups milk

1 5 1/2-ounce package vanilla instant pudding mix

12 ounces whipped topping

Heat margarine, brown sugar and pecans in saucepan until bubbly, stirring constantly. Spoon into tart shells. Bake at 450 degrees for 5 minutes. Cool. Blend milk and pudding mix in bowl. Reserve 1 cup pudding. Spoon remaining pudding into tart shells. Blend reserved pudding with whipped topping. Spread over tarts. Yield: 12 servings.

Approx Per Serving:
Cal 403; Prot 5 g; Carbo 27 g; T Fat 23 g; Chol 6 mg; Potas 194 mg; Sod 232 mg.

Wanda Luton, Florida

REFRIGERATION CHART

Food	Refrigerate	Freeze
Beef steaks	1-2 days	6-12 months
Beef roasts	1-2 days	6-12 months
Corned beef	7 days	2 weeks
Pork chops	1-2 days	3-4 months
Pork roasts	1-2 days	4-8 months
Fresh sausage	1-2 days	1-2 months
Smoked sausage	7 days	Not recommended
Cured ham	5-7 days	1-2 months
Canned ham	1 year	Not recommended
Ham slice	3 days	1-2 months
Bacon	7 days	2-4 months
Veal cutlets	1-2 days	6-9 months
Stew meat	1-2 days	3-4 months
Ground meat	1-2 days	3-4 months
Luncheon meats	3-5 days	Not recommended
Frankfurters	7 days	1 month
Whole chicken	1-2 days	12 months
Chicken pieces	1-2 days	9 months

Freezing Tips

- Date all items before placing them in the freezer.
- Frozen canned hams become watery and soft when thawed. Processed meats have a high salt content which speeds rancidity when thawed.
- Do not freeze stuffed chickens or turkeys. The stuffing may suffer bacterial contamination during the lengthy thawing process.
- Partially thawed food which still has ice crystals in the package can be safely refrozen. A safer test is to determine if the surface temperature is 40° F. or lower.

SUBSTITUTION CHART

	Instead of	Use
Baking	1 teaspoon baking powder	1/4 teaspoon soda plus 1/2 teaspoon cream of tartar
	1 tablespoon cornstarch (for thickening)	2 tablespoons flour or 1 tablespoon tapioca
	1 cup sifted all-purpose flour	1 cup plus 2 tablespoons sifted cake flour
	1 cup sifted cake flour	1 cup minus 2 tablespoons sifted all-purpose flour
	1 cup dry bread crumbs	3/4 cup cracker crumbs
Dairy	1 cup buttermilk	1 cup sour milk or 1 cup yogurt
	1 cup heavy cream	3/4 cup skim milk plus 1/3 cup butter
	1 cup light cream	7/8 cup skim milk plus 3 tablespoons butter
	1 cup sour cream	7/8 cup sour milk plus 3 tablespoons butter
	1 cup sour milk	1 cup milk plus 1 tablespoon vinegar or lemon juice or 1 cup buttermilk
Seasoning	1 teaspoon allspice	1/2 teaspoon cinnamon plus 1/8 teaspoon cloves
	1 cup catsup	1 cup tomato sauce plus 1/2 cup sugar plus 2 tablespoons vinegar
	1 clove of garlic	1/8 teaspoon garlic powder or 1/8 teaspoon instant minced garlic or 3/4 teaspoon garlic salt or 5 drops of liquid garlic
	1 teaspoon Italian spice	1/4 teaspoon each oregano, basil, thyme, rosemary plus dash of cayenne
	1 teaspoon lemon juice	1/2 teaspoon vinegar
	1 tablespoon mustard	1 teaspoon dry mustard
	1 medium onion	1 tablespoon dried minced onion or 1 teaspoon onion powder
Sweet	1 1-ounce square chocolate	1/4 cup cocoa plus 1 teaspoon shortening
	1 2/3 ounces semisweet chocolate	1 ounce unsweetened chocolate plus 4 teaspoons granulated sugar
	1 cup honey	1 to 1 1/4 cups sugar plus 1/4 cup liquid or 1 cup corn syrup or molasses
	1 cup granulated sugar	1 cup packed brown sugar or 1 cup corn syrup, molasses or honey minus 1/4 cup liquid

EQUIVALENT CHART

	When the recipe calls for	Use
Baking	1/2 cup butter	4 ounces
	2 cups butter	1 pound
	4 cups all-purpose flour	1 pound
	4 1/2 to 5 cups sifted cake flour	1 pound
	1 square chocolate	1 ounce
	1 cup semisweet chocolate chips	6 ounces
	4 cups marshmallows	1 pound
	2 1/4 cups packed brown sugar	1 pound
	4 cups confectioners' sugar	1 pound
	2 cups granulated sugar	1 pound
Cereal – Bread	1 cup fine dry bread crumbs	4 to 5 slices
	1 cup soft bread crumbs	2 slices
	1 cup small bread cubes	2 slices
	1 cup fine cracker crumbs	28 saltines
	1 cup fine graham cracker crumbs	15 crackers
	1 cup vanilla wafer crumbs	22 wafers
	1 cup crushed cornflakes	3 cups uncrushed
	4 cups cooked macaroni	8 ounces uncooked
	3 1/2 cups cooked rice	1 cup uncooked
Dairy	1 cup shredded cheese	4 ounces
	1 cup cottage cheese	8 ounces
	1 cup sour cream	8 ounces
	1 cup whipped cream	1/2 cup heavy cream
	2/3 cup evaporated milk	1 small can
	1 2/3 cups evaporated milk	1 13-ounce can
Fruit	4 cups sliced or chopped apples	4 medium
	1 cup mashed bananas	3 medium
	2 cups pitted cherries	4 cups unpitted
	3 cups shredded coconut	8 ounces
	4 cups cranberries	1 pound
	1 cup pitted dates	1 8-ounce package
	1 cup candied fruit	1 8-ounce package
	3 to 4 tablespoons lemon juice plus 1 tablespoon grated lemon rind	1 lemon
	1/3 cup orange juice plus 2 teaspoons grated orange rind	1 orange
	4 cups sliced peaches	8 medium
	2 cups pitted prunes	1 12-ounce package
	3 cups raisins	1 15-ounce package

When the recipe calls for	Use
Meats 4 cups chopped cooked chicken 3 cups chopped cooked meat 2 cups cooked ground meat	1 5-pound chicken 1 pound, cooked 1 pound, cooked
Nuts 1 cup chopped nuts	4 ounces shelled 1 pound unshelled
Vegetables 2 cups cooked green beans 2¹/₂ cups lima beans or red beans 4 cups shredded cabbage 1 cup grated carrot 8 ounces fresh mushrooms 1 cup chopped onion 4 cups sliced or chopped potatoes 2 cups canned tomatoes	¹/₂ pound fresh or 1 16-ounce can 1 cup dried, cooked 1 pound 1 large 1 4-ounce can 1 large 4 medium 1 16-ounce can

Measurement Equivalents

1 tablespoon = 3 teaspoons 2 tablespoons = 1 ounce 4 tablespoons = ¹/₄ cup 5¹/₃ tablespoons = ¹/₃ cup 8 tablespoons = ¹/₂ cup 12 tablespoons = ³/₄ cup 16 tablespoons = 1 cup 1 cup = 8 ounces or ¹/₂ pint 4 cups = 1 quart 4 quarts = 1 gallon	1 6¹/₂ to 8-ounce can = 1 cup 1 10¹/₂ to 12-ounce can = 1¹/₄ cups 1 14 to 16-ounce can = 1³/₄ cups 1 16 to 17-ounce can = 2 cups 1 18 to 20-ounce can = 2¹/₂ cups 1 20-ounce can = 3¹/₂ cups 1 46 to 51-ounce can = 5³/₄ cups 1 6¹/₂ to 7¹/₂-pound can or Number 10 can = 12 to 13 cups

Metric Equivalents

Liquid	Dry
1 teaspoon = 5 milliliters 1 tablespoon = 15 milliliters 1 fluid ounce = 30 milliliters 1 cup = 250 milliliters 1 pint = 500 milliliters	1 quart = 1 liter 1 ounce = 30 grams 1 pound = 450 grams 2.2 pounds = 1 kilogram

NOTE: The metric measures are approximate benchmarks for purposes of home food preparation.

DIETARY FIBER IN FOODS

		Amount	Weight (grams)	Fiber (grams)
Breads	Graham crackers	2 squares	14.2	0.4
	Pumpernickel bread	3/4 slice	24	1.4
	Rye bread	1 slice	25	1.7
	Whole wheat bread	1 slice	25	1.9
	Whole wheat crackers	6 crackers	19.8	2.1
	Whole wheat roll	3/4 roll	21	1.5
Fruit	Apple	1/2 large	83	2.1
	Apricots	2	72	1.4
	Banana	1/2 medium	54	1.1
	Blackberries	3/4 cup	108	7.3
	Cantaloupe	1 cup	160	1.6
	Cherries	10 large	68	1.0
	Dates, dried	2	18	1.5
	Figs, dried	1 medium	20	2.2
	Grapes, green	10	50	0.6
	Grapefruit	1/2	87	1.1
	Honeydew	1 cup	170	1.8
	Orange	1 small	78	1.9
	Peach	1 medium	100	1.7
	Pear	1/2 medium	82	2.3
	Pineapple	1/2	78	1.2
	Plums	3 small	85	1.7
	Prunes, dried	2	15	1.4
	Raisins	1 1/2 tbsp.	14	0.8
	Strawberries	1 cup	143	3.7
	Tangerine	1 large	101	2.0
	Watermelon	1 cup	160	0.6
Grains	All Bran	1/3 cup	28	8.5
	Bran Chex	1/2 cup	21	3.9
	Corn Bran	1/2 cup	21	4.0
	Corn Flakes	3/4 cup	21	0.4
	Grapenuts Flakes	2/3 cup	21	1.4
	Grapenuts	3 tbsp.	21	1.4
	Oatmeal	3/4 pkg.	21	2.3
	Shredded Wheat	1 biscuit	21	2.2
	Wheaties	3/4 cup	21	2.0

		Amount	Weight (grams)	Fiber (grams)
Rice	Rice, brown, cooked	1/3 cup	65	1.1
	Rice, white, cooked	1/3 cup	68	0.2
Meat, Milk, Eggs	Beef	1 ounce	28	0.0
	Cheese	3/4 ounce	21	0.0
	Chicken/Turkey	1 ounce	28	0.0
	Cold cuts/Frankfurters	1 ounce	28	0.0
	Eggs	3 large	99	0.0
	Fish	2 ounces	56	0.0
	Ice cream	1 ounce	28	0.0
	Milk	1 cup	240	0.0
	Pork	1 ounce	28	0.0
	Yogurt	5 ounces	140	0.0
Vegetables	Beans, green	1/2 cup	64	1.5
	Beans, string	1/2 cup	55	2.1
	Beets	1/2 cup	85	1.7
	Broccoli	1/2 cup	93	3.1
	Brussels sprouts	1/2 cup	78	3.5
	Cabbage	1/2 cup	85	2.0
	Carrots	1/2 cup	78	2.5
	Cauliflower	1/2 cup	90	2.3
	Celery	1/2 cup	60	1.0
	Cucumber	1/2 cup	70	0.8
	Eggplant	1/2 cup	100	3.4
	Lentils, cooked	1/2 cup	100	5.1
	Lettuce	1 cup	55	0.7
	Mushrooms	1/2 cup	35	0.6
	Onions	1/2 cup	58	0.9
	Potato, baked	1/2 medium	75	1.8
	Radishes	1/2 cup	58	1.3
	Spinach, fresh	1 cup	55	1.8
	Sweet potato, baked	1/2 medium	75	2.3
	Tomato	1 small	100	1.5
	Turnip greens	1/2 cup	93	2.9
	Winter squash	1/2 cup	120	3.4
	Zucchini	1/2 cup	65	0.7

MICROWAVE TIPS

- Always choose the minimum cooking time. Remember, food continues to cook after it is removed from the microwave.
- Keep your microwave clean. Built-up grease or food spatters can slow cooking times.
- When poaching or frying an egg in a browning dish, always prick the center of the yolk with a fork to keep the egg from exploding.
- Do not try to hard-cook eggs *in the shell* in a microwave. They will build up pressure and burst.
- Do not use metal dishes or aluminum foil except as specifically recommended by the manufacturer of your microwave.
- Never use a foil tray over 3/4 inch deep in your microwave.
- When heating TV-style dinners, remove the foil cover, then place tray back in carton. Food will heat only from the top.
- Be sure to prick potatoes before baking to allow steam to escape.
- Cut a small slit in pouch-packed frozen foods before heating in microwave to allow steam to escape.
- When placing more than one food item in microwave, arrange foods in a circle near edges of oven.
- Cover foods that need to be steamed or tenderized.
- Do not try to pop popcorn without a microwave-approved corn popper.

Did You Know You Can...?
(Use HIGH setting for the following unless otherwise indicated.)

- Use your microwave oven to melt chocolate, to soften cream cheese and to soften or melt butter.
- Roast shelled nuts for 6 to 10 minutes, stirring frequently.
- Peel fruit or tomatoes by placing in 1 cup hot water. Microwave for 30 to 45 seconds; remove skins easily.
- Plump dried fruit by placing in a dish with 1 to 2 teaspoons water. Cover tightly with plastic wrap. Microwave for 1/2 to 1 1/2 minutes.
- Precook barbecued ribs or chicken in the microwave until almost done, then place on the grill to sear and add a charcoal flavor.
- Soften brown sugar by placing in a dish with a slice of bread or apple and microwave for 30 to 45 seconds, stirring once.
- Dry bread for crumbs or croutons. Place cubed or crumbled bread on paper towels. Microwave for 6 to 7 minutes, stirring occasionally.
- Warm baby food or baby bottles by removing metal lid and microwaving for 10 to 20 seconds. Be sure to test temperature before feeding baby.
- Freshen chips and crackers by microwaving for 15 to 30 seconds. Let stand for 2 to 3 minutes.
- Dry herbs by placing on paper towels and microwaving for 2 to 3 minutes or until herbs are dry.
- Ripen an avocado by microwaving on LOW for 2 to 4 minutes.

COOKING MEAT AND POULTRY

ROASTING
- Use tender cuts of beef, veal, pork or lamb and young birds.
- Place meat fat side up, or poultry breast side up, on rack in foil-lined shallow roasting pan. Do not add water; do not cover.
- Insert meat thermometer in center of thickest part of meat, being careful that end does not touch bone, fat or gristle.
- Roast at 300 to 350 degrees to desired degree of doneness.

BROILING
- Use tender beef steaks, lamb chops, sliced ham, ground meats and poultry quarters or halves. Fresh pork should be broiled slowly to insure complete cooking in center. Steaks and chops should be at least 1/2 inch thick.
- Preheat oven to "Broil". Place meat on rack in foil-lined broiler pan.
- Place meat on oven rack 2 to 5 inches from the heat source, with thicker meat placed the greater distance. Brush poultry with butter.
- Broil until top side is browned; season with salt and pepper.
- Turn; brown second side. Season and serve at once.

PAN BROILING
- Use the same cuts as suitable for broiling.
- Place skillet or griddle over medium-high heat. Preheat until a drop of water dances on the surface.
- Place meat in skillet; reduce heat to medium. Do not add water or cover. The cold meat will stick at first, but as it browns it will loosen. If juices start to cook out of the meat, increase heat slightly.
- When meat is brown on one side, turn and brown second side.

PAN FRYING
- Use comparatively thin pieces of meat, meat that has been tenderized by pounding or scoring, meat that is breaded and chicken parts.
- Place skillet over medium-high heat. Add a small amount of shortening—2 tablespoons will usually be sufficient.
- When shortening is hot, add meat or poultry. Cook as in pan broiling.

BRAISING
- Use for less tender cuts of meat or older birds. You can also braise pork chops, steaks and cutlets; veal chops, steaks and cutlets; and chicken legs and thighs.
- Brown meat on all sides as in pan frying. Season with salt and pepper.
- Add a small amount of water—or none if sufficient juices have already cooked out of the meat. Cover tightly.
- Reduce heat to low. Cook until tender, turning occasionally. Meats will cook in their own juices.

COOKING IN LIQUID
- Use less tender cuts of meat and stewing chickens. Browning of large cuts or whole birds is optional, but it does develop flavor and improve the color.
- Add water or stock to cover meat. Simmer, covered, until tender.
- Add vegetables to allow time to cook without becoming mushy.

CALORIE CHART

Almonds, shelled, 1/4 cup 213
Apples: 1 med 70
   chopped, 1/2 cup 30
   juice, 1 cup 117
Applesauce, 1/2 cup: sweetened 115
   unsweetened 50
Apricots: canned, 1/2 cup 110
   dried, 10 halves 100
   fresh, 3 55
   nectar, 1 cup 140
Asparagus: canned, 1/2 cup 18
   fresh, 6 spears 19
Avocado, 1 med 265
Bacon, crisp-cooked, 2 slices 90
Banana, 1 med 100
Beans, 1/2 cup: baked 160
   dried 350
   green 20
   lima 95
   soy 95
Bean sprouts, 1/2 cup 18
Beef, cooked, 3 oz:
   broiled, sirloin steak 330
   roasted, heel of round 165
   roasted, rib 375
Beer, 12 oz 150
Beets, cooked, 1/2 cup 40
Biscuit, from mix, 1 90
Bologna, all meat, 3 oz 235
Bread: 1 roll 85
   white, 1 slice 65
   whole wheat, 1 slice 55
Bread crumbs, dry, 1 cup 390
Broccoli, cooked, 1/2 cup 20
Butter, 1 tbsp 100
Buttermilk, 1 cup 90
Cabbage, 1/2 cup: cooked 15
   fresh, shredded 10
Cake, 1/12 cake: angel food 140
   devil's food 195
   yellow 200
Candy, 1 oz: caramel 115
   chocolate, sweet 145
   hard candy 110
   marshmallows 90
Cantaloupe, 1/2 med 60
Carrots: cooked, 1/2 cup 23
   fresh, 1 med 20
Catsup, 1 tbsp 18
Cauliflower: cooked, 1/2 cup 13
   fresh, 1/2 lb 60
Celery, chopped, 1/2 cup 8
Cereals, 1/2 cup: bran flakes 53

cornflakes 50
oatmeal, cooked 65
Cheese: American, 1 oz 105
   Cheddar, 1 oz 113
   cottage: creamed, 1/2 cup 130
     uncreamed, 1/2 cup 85
   cream, 1 oz 107
   mozzarella, 1 oz 80
   Parmesan, 1 oz 110
   Velveeta, 1 oz 84
Cherries, 1/2 cup: canned, sour 53
   fresh, sweet 40
Chicken, cooked, 4 oz:
   broiled 155
   canned, boned 230
   roasted, dark meat 210
   roasted, light meat 207
Chilies, fresh, 8 oz: green 62
   red 108
Chili powder, 1 tbsp 51
Chocolate, baking, 1 oz 143
Cocoa mix, 1 oz 115
Cocoa, unsweetened, 1/3 cup 120
Coconut, shredded, 1/4 cup 166
Coffee 0
Corn, 1/2 cup: cream-style 100
   whole kernel 85
Corn bread, 1x4-in. piece 125
Corn chips, 1 oz 130
Cornmeal, 1/2 cup 264
Cornstarch, 1 tbsp 29
Crab meat, 3 oz: canned 85
   fresh 80
Crackers: graham, 1 square 28
   Ritz, 1 17
   saltine, 1 square 13
Cracker crumbs, 1/2 cup 281
Cranberries: fresh, 1/2 lb 100
   juice, cocktail, 1 cup 163
   sauce, 1/2 cup 190
Cream, 1 tbsp: half and half 20
   heavy 55
   light 30
Creamer, nondairy, 1 tsp 10
Cucumber, 1 med 30
Dates, chopped, 1/2 cup 244
Eggs: 1 whole, large 80
   1 white 17
   1 yolk 59
Eggplant, cooked, 1/2 cup 19
Fish sticks, 5 200
Flour, 1 cup:
   all-purpose 420

rye		286
whole wheat		400
Fruit cocktail, canned, 1/2 cup		98
Garlic, 1 clove		2
Gelatin, unflavored, 1 env.		25
Grapes: fresh, 1/2 cup		35-50
juice, 1 cup		170
Grapefruit: fresh, 1/2 med		60
juice, unsweetened, 1 cup		100

Ground beef, cooked, 3 oz:
    lean 185
    regular 245
Haddock, fried, 3 oz 140
Ham, cooked, 3 oz:
    boiled 200
    country-style 335
    cured, lean 160
    roasted, fresh 320
Honey, 1 tbsp. 65
Ice cream, 1/2 cup 135
Ice milk, 1/2 cup 96
Jams and preserves, 1 tbsp 54
Jellies, 1 tbsp 55
Jell-O, 1/2 cup 80
Lamb, cooked, 3 oz:
    broiled, rib chop 175
    roasted, leg 185
Lemonade, sweetened, 1 cup 110
Lemon juice, 1 tbsp 4
Lentils, cooked, 1/2 cup 168
Lettuce, 1 head 40
Liver, 2 oz: beef, fried 130
    chicken, simmered 88
Lobster, 2 oz 55
Macaroni, cooked, 1/2 cup 90
Mango, 1 fresh 134
Margarine, 1 tbsp 100
Mayonnaise, 1 tbsp 100
Milk, 1 cup:
    condensed 982
    evaporated 385
    nonfat dry 251
    skim 89
    2% 145
    whole 160
Mushrooms: canned, 1/2 cup 20
    fresh, 1 lb. 123
Mustard, prepared, 1 tbsp:
    brown 13
    yellow 10
Nectarine, 1 fresh 30
Noodles: egg, cooked, 1/2 cup 100
    fried, chow mein, 2 oz 275

Oil, cooking, salad, 1 tbsp 120
Okra, cooked, 8 pods 25
Olives: green, 3 lg 15
    ripe, 2 lg 15
Onion:
    chopped, 1/2 cup 32
    green, 6 20
Oranges: 1 med 65
    juice, 1 cup 115
Oysters, 1/2 cup 80
Peaches: canned, 1/2 cup 100
    dried, 1/2 cup 210
    1 med 35
Peanuts, roasted, 1 cup 420
Peanut butter, 1 tbsp 100
Pears: canned, 1/2 cup 97
    dried, 1/2 cup 214
    fresh, 1 med 100
Peas, 1/2 cup:
    black-eyed 70
    green, canned 83
    green, frozen 69
Pecans, chopped, 1/2 cup 400
Peppers, sweet. 1 med: green 14
    red 19
Perch, white, 4 oz 50
Pickles: dill, 1 lg 15
    sweet, 1 med 30
Pie, 1/6 pie:
    apple 420
    cherry 402
    custard 330
    pumpkin 321
Pie crust, mix, 1 crust 626
Pimento, canned, 1 med 10
Pineapple: canned, 1/2 cup 90
    fresh, 1/2 cup 36
    juice, 1 cup 135
Plums: canned, 3 101
    fresh, 1 med 30
Popcorn, popped, 1 cup: plain 23
    with oil and salt 40
Pork, cooked, lean:
    broiled, chop, 3.5 oz 260
    roasted, Boston Butt, 4 oz 280
    roasted, loin, 4 oz 290
Potato chips, 10 med 114
Potatoes, white:
    baked, with skin, 1 sm 93
    boiled, 1 sm 70
    French-fried, 10 pieces 175
    hashed brown, 1/2 cup 177
    mashed, 1/2 cup 90

Potatoes, sweet:
   baked, 1 med 155
   candied, 1 med 295
   canned, 1/2 cup 110
Prunes: dried, cooked, 1/2 cup 137
   fresh, 1 lg 19
   juice, 1 cup 197
Puddings, instant, prepared,
    1/2 cup:
   banana 175
   butterscotch 175
   chocolate 200
   lemon 180
Puddings, pie fillings, prepared,
    1/2 cup:
   banana 165
   butterscotch 190
   chocolate 190
   lemon 125
Pumpkin, canned, 1/2 cup 38
Raisins, 1/2 cup 231
Rice, cooked, 1/2 cup:
   brown 100
   minute 105
   white 90
Salad dressings, 1 tbsp:
   blue cheese 75
   French 70
   Italian 83
   mayonnaise 100
   mayonnaise-type 65
   Russian 75
   Thousand Island 80
Salami, cooked, 2 oz 180
Salmon, 4 oz: canned 180
   steak 220
Sardines, canned, 3 oz 75
Sauces, 1 tbsp: barbecue 17
   hot pepper 3
   soy 9
   tartar 74
   white, med 215
   Worcestershire 15
Sauerkraut, 1/2 cup 21
Sausage, cooked, 2 oz 260
Sherbet, 1/2 cup 130
Shrimp: canned, 4 oz 130
   cooked, 3 oz 50
Soft drinks, 1 cup 100
Soup, condensed, 1 can:
   chicken with rice 116
   cream of celery 215

   cream of chicken 235
   cream of mushroom 331
   tomato 220
   vegetable-beef 198
Sour cream, 1/2 cup 240
Spaghetti, cooked, 1/2 cup 80
Spinach: cooked, 1/2 cup 20
   fresh, 1/2 lb 60
Squash: summer, 1/2 cup 15
   winter, 1/2 cup 65
Strawberries, fresh, 1/2 cup 23
Sugar: brown, 1/2 cup 410
   confectioners', 1/2 cup 240
   granulated, 1/2 cup 385
   1 tbsp. 48
Syrups, 1 tbsp: chocolate 50
   corn 58
   maple 50
Taco shell, 1 shell 50
Tomatoes: canned, 1/2 cup 25
   fresh, 1 med 40
   juice, 1 cup 45
   paste, 6-oz 150
   sauce, 8-oz 34
Toppings, 1 tbsp: caramel 70
   chocolate fudge 65
   Cool Whip 14
   Dream Whip 8
   strawberry 60
Tortilla, corn, 1 65
Tuna, canned, 4 oz:
   in oil 230
   in water 144
Turkey, roasted, 4 oz:
   dark meat 230
   light meat 200
Veal, cooked, 3 oz:
   broiled, cutlet 185
   roasted 230
Vegetable juice cocktail, 1 cup 43
Vinegar, 1 tbsp 2
Waffles, 1 130
Walnuts, chopped, 1/2 cup 410
Water chestnuts, 1/2 cup 25
Watermelon, fresh, 1/2 cup 26
Wheat germ, 1 tbsp 29
Yeast: cake, 1 oz 24
   dry, 1 oz 80
Yogurt, 1 cup: plain 153
   plain, skim milk 123
   plain whole milk 139
   with fruit 260

INDEX

ADD TO YOUR COOKBOOK COLLECTION

The *Animaland Cookbook* compiled by Dixie (Mrs. Tom T.) Hall is more than just a cookbook. It is the united effort of people from all walks of life joining hands to benefit All Creatures Great and Small, people and animals.

It is a "purrfectly" "doggone" good collection of favorite recipes which will grace any kitchen and which will make a "tasteful" gift for any occasion. And there are exciting photographs of stars—often with their pets!

All proceeds from the sale of this book will benefit Animaland, a thirty-two acre complex located near Nashville, Tennessee.

The Animaland Cookbook contains recipes from Dolly Parton, Gary Morris, Hank Williams, Jr., George Jones, Waylon Jennings, Minnie Pearl, The Gatlin Brothers, Johnny Cash, President and Rosalyn Carter, Michael Martin Murphey, Jeanne Pruett, Kenny Rogers, Ernest Tubb, Tanya Tucker, The Statler Brothers, Dottie West, Barbara Mandrell and many, many more.

ORDER FORM — *Animaland Cookbook*

To order your copy of the *Animaland Cookbook* please send **$11.95** per book to:

**Animaland
P.O. Box 1591
Franklin, TN 37065
Tel. (615) 794-8679**

Name _____

Address _____

City _____

State _____

Zip _____

Please send me _____ copy(s) of the *Animaland Cookbook*.

ADD TO YOUR COOKBOOK COLLECTION

Laurels to the Cook is more than 350 home-tested recipes from the Laurel Mountains of Western Pennsylvania. Named best community cookbook by *Pennsylvania* magazine, this 224-page cookbook is published by Talus Rock Girl Scout Council. Special features of *Laurels to the Cook* include a section of chef's favorites from local restaurants and Girl Scout centers worldwide along with pen-and-ink sketches of local landmarks. A lovely watercolor of Mountain Laurel, Pennsylvania's state flower, graces the full-color cover.

To order this award-winning cookbook, please return this form with your check for **$9.00** per book (state sales tax included) plus **$2.00** shipping and handling to Talus Rock Girl Scout Council Inc., 612 Locust Street, Johnstown, PA 15901.

ORDER FORM   *Laurels to the Cook*

To order your copy of the *Laurels to the Cook* please send **$9.00** per book plus **$2.00** shipping and handling to:

Talus Rock Girl Scout Council, Inc
612 Locust Street
Johnstown, PA 15901

Name _____

Address _____

City _____

State _____

Zip _____

   Please send me _____ copy(s) of *Laurels to the Cook*.